FOREWORD

This second book by Sandy Brownjohn will interest all teachers of English. The writing she has drawn from her young pupils over the last few years has been remarkable – and often astonishing – for its quality and inventiveness. One important part of her method is a repertoire of verbal classroom games. In these chapters she describes these games, and shows how they can be used productively.

As in her first book, she includes a good sampling of her pupils' work. In any school one would have to call these young writers of hers (around eleven years old) outstandingly gifted. And yet she succeeds not just with the odd pupil – whom we might think had that natural bent – but with a big proportion of her class. And everybody in her class shares in the benefits, because all are able to share and enjoy the activity.

Whatever is going on here, it is certainly worth very close examination by all English teachers.

A first reaction to Sandy Brownjohn's success is sometimes a negative one: her results are so striking that we might feel, automatically, there must be something wrong with them, or with her methods. We might even feel it is not natural that such young children should write with such sophistication.

But have we any notion of what would be natural? I think most of us would hesitate to call the situation in any classroom 'natural'. We actually have no idea what any child's real abilities are – we only know they are much greater than the child ever brings into play. And we have no idea, either, what kind of teaching would engage these hidden real abilities and bring them to full flower. I know – I have felt it myself – the teacher's pang of despair when he glimpses a pupil's real potential, and knows there is no way of catching hold of it and developing it, because few teachers, if any, know how to, it is beyond what ordinary educational methods are designed to deal with, and even, in a way, beyond what our society can accept. One is amazed to read how the Kazars are said to have executed any of their members who showed unusual intelligence, yet we have all felt the natural human resistance against superior cleverness, even in those we are trying to teach.

My own view of the contrast between a child's hidden abilities and the ones he or she shows in class was sharpened by an experience I had while teaching in a secondary modern school. There was no question, in that school, of the children deriving any academic advantage from their home background. Two or three times a week I took a class of backward boys. I'm not sure how they were singled out, but our lesson was meant to be maths. It always began with a laborious mass recitation of the multiplication tables, and was then filled up by anything I could invent. It seemed to me that all these boys were bright enough, but were simply non-survivors in the extreme climate of the classroom. None of them could give the answer to 3 × 3. After a hesitant wrong guess, there would be a free-for-all of wrong guesses, until some random hit got it right.

Seeing how perversely they avoided the correct answer, it struck me that what they lacked was not so much mathematical ability as confidence in their own brains. I explained this to them as a slight temporary flaw, and persuaded them that mathematical ability is equal in all people, because it takes its instructions direct from the physical chemistry of our body, which is a phenomenal genius and always gets everything miraculously right. My story was quite long, with digressions about the subconscious mind, but it evidently persuaded them that all they needed to do, when I gave them a mental sum, was to trust the first thing that came into their heads. 'Your real brain is moving so fast,' I assured them, 'that if you hesitate even for a second you'll miss it. It will have gone past like an express train through a station. Then you'll have to catch the next slow stopping one along and that will be wrong.' I asked them to yell out an answer – without thinking – as soon as I gave them the sum.

For the remaining ten minutes of the lesson, it worked. I asked simple multiplications (I wrote the answers out on paper first – the highest was 19 × 19 – so that I could seem to be in on the gift of instant certainty), and every answer jumped back at me correct. I wondered if I had chanced on some revolutionary teaching method. By the end of the lesson the boys were wildly excited – and bemused. Neither they nor I knew what to make of it. Our problem solved itself, however. By the next lesson, the miracle was over. Their idea of their own limitations had moved in the night, and sealed off the escape route I had opened, and was now on guard. I was never able to open it again.

I've often remembered those boys, because in the act of writing, especially of writing verse, one is always convinced that what appears on the page is only a distorted fraction of what, somewhere or other inside us, wanted to appear, and would have appeared, too, if only we knew how to listen to it more subtly and widely and deeply, and record it more boldly. The progress of any writer is marked by those moments when he manages to outwit his own inner police system which tells him what is permissible, what is possible, what is 'him'. Writers have invented all kinds of 'games' to get past their own censorship. Dickens had to wear a certain ring. Hart Crane played jazz at top volume. Schiller invented free association.

'Inspiration' is a poor word for those occasions, and perhaps in most cases a wrong word. One thing such times have in common is a willingness to relax expectation, and to experiment, to let flow – a willingness to put on masks and to play.

Which brings us back to the games which Sandy Brownjohn uses in her writing classes. Her pupils produce what they want to produce: startling poetic combinations of words and ideas, startling complete patterns of poetic sense. But these effects are really incidental. These writers are simultaneously doing something else, something which must be much more valuable to them. They are practising techniques of self-exploration and productive play, by which I mean free, searching play of the mind among its galleries of memory, imagination and perception.

It is a multiple, unselfconscious exercise of what has come to be known as lateral thinking. Though it is applied here, in an intensive way, to imaginative writing, it is at bottom the same technique which is becoming popular, because so successful, in the brainstorming creative idea sessions of working scientists, engineers, and in all activities that depend on flexible adaptation to new facts and needs, and a steady influx of new and better solutions. It is a natural technique, too – it is the one the brain itself uses in subconscious work and in sleep, to solve the problems of daily life.

And as a system it is based on assumptions quite opposite to the minimal expectations of our educational system. It is based on the confidence that we have an inexhaustible capacity for producing the answers to problems, and that there is only one problem, how to tap that capacity at will, and that we have answers to that problem too.

But the incidental fruits of Sandy Brownjohn's method are also very great. Reading her account of her classes, we can see that while her pupils are focusing all their excitement on the one ambition, to write their poem, they are becoming, in the process and almost unwittingly, sophisticated verbalists, with large vocabularies which they use with discrimination and zest; they are becoming skilled manipulators of sentence structure and phrasing, and strongly motivated critical readers. In making their bid for the three minute forty second mile, so to speak, they are running four minute miles just for training. Most of the aims of English teaching have been encompassed in the single task.

In all this, no teacher will fail to give Sandy Brownjohn her due. It is a remarkable personal achievement for her, to have fitted so many novel approaches together, and to have brought off, year after year, such a triumph of sheer teaching. But even when we have given full credit to her classroom skills, there still remain those practical solid tools of her methods, which are for anybody to use.

Perhaps they leave us with only one problem. Once children have come so far, so fast, where else can they go, in English lessons? How can this beginning be hung on to and developed? Surely everything that has been uncovered in this way will soon be smothered by conventional English teaching. What kind of English teaching will not smother it?

That problem still has to be solved, but it is one which has not yet been consciously tackled. Sandy Brownjohn herself has to say goodbye to her eleven-year-olds at the end of each year.

But whatever comes after it, these early exercises, this precociously developed ability, in lateral thinking in words, imaginative ideas and perceptions, can surely only be good. The pupil has been given a whole kit of techniques for opening his or her own mind, quite apart from that pleasure and confidence in the uses of language, and a taste for literature. This is surely as crucial as the teaching of memory and recall, and of concentration in productive effort – two fundamental, essential skills without which education cannot properly start (without which it becomes little more than institutionalised baby-sitting).

These 'games', which Sandy Brownjohn has collected here, seem to me the most serious kind of business.

Ted Hughes

CONTENTS

FOR
MY FAMILY,
ALL MY FRIENDS
AND ALL MY PUPILS

What Rhymes with 'Secret'?

Teaching children to write poetry

Sandy Brownjohn

With a Foreword by Ted Hughes

HODDER AND STOUGHTON

LONDON SYDNEY AUCKLAND TORONTO

British Library Cataloguing in Publication Data

Brownjohn, Sandy
 What rhymes with 'Secret'?
 1. Poetic – Study and teaching –
  Great Britain
 2. English literature – Study and teaching –
  Great Britain
 I. Title
 808.1   PN1101

ISBN 0 340 28271 1

First published 1982
Sixth impression 1987

Phototypeset in Linotron Palatino by
Rowland Phototypesetting Ltd,
Bury St Edmunds, Suffolk
Printed and bound in Great Britain for
Hodder and Stoughton Educational,
a division of Hodder and Stoughton Ltd,
Mill Road, Dunton Green, Sevenoaks, Kent,
by Biddles Ltd, Guildford and King's Lynn

AUTHOR'S NOTE

This book is a follow-up to my first, *Does It Have To Rhyme?* (Hodder and Stoughton 1980) and is again meant as a handbook for teachers, to be used primarily with the 9–15 age group. It is conceived more as a complement to the first and not necessarily as an extension in difficulty. It is based completely on my approach and experience in teaching children to write poetry and is offered to other teachers in the hope that they may find something of use to them. I do not claim that my approach is the only one that works and many people may disagree with much of what I say, but if it only provokes discussion at least it will have achieved one purpose, namely that of making us question how we teach writing and its value to society.

I should like to point out that I feel that good writing by anyone cannot be achieved 'overnight', it takes a lot of time and practice and teachers should not be discouraged if the first results do not match up to expectations. I teach children aged 9–11 years, the examples in this book are by them, and I consider that it takes at least a year of exposing them to all the different techniques and ideas at my disposal before they begin to be able to write properly, with full confidence and in their own personal style.

Where the symbol (YWW) appears beside a child's name this indicates that the poems were written at the ILEA Young Writers' Workshop which I have been running with Frank Flynn for over three years for children aged 10–13.

Sandy Brownjohn

ACKNOWLEDGMENTS

'Ship in A Bottle' by Miles Greene was an award winner in the W. H. Smith Children's Literary Competition 1979, and was published in *Children As Writers* (Heinemann 1980).

'The Making of the Tiger' by Nadya Kassam, 'Jack-In-A-Box' by Miles Greene and 'Suburbia' by Ben Owen were award winners in the W. H. Smith Children's Literary Competition 1980 and were published in *Children as Writers* (Heinemann 1981).

'Alcohol' by Helen Alexander was an award winner in the W. H. Smith Children's Literary Competition 1981 and was published in *Children as Writers* (Heinemann 1982).

Many of the poems were published in the booklets *Crossing Lines* (1978) and *Second Crossing* (1980, Fitzjohn's Imprint).

Chapter 19, *Learning Poems by Heart*, first appeared as an article in *Junior Education* (May 1980, Vol. 4, No 5).

My thanks and gratitude to Homerton College, Cambridge, for my term as an Associate, when I wrote this book, and to the ILEA for granting me Leave of Absence for that time. Very special thanks to Jessie Ball whose encouragement and assistance at that time were invaluable.

Lastly, continuing thanks to David Wallis-Jones, my long-suffering headmaster, to all the poets, friends and family who have supported me at all times, and, of course, to the children who have made the whole thing so exciting.

S.L.B.

1 POETRY GAMES

There are many games that can be used to encourage children to play with words and explore their possibilities. Some of these were set out in my first book, *Does It Have To Rhyme?* Here are some more games which are specifically to do with the writing of poetry and can be played over and over again. Each time the result will be different.

Lucky Dip

This game can be used as a warming-up exercise or as a whole lesson. The children make up perhaps ten lines of poetry which are written down leaving a space between each one. The lines may hang together as a poem in its own right, or they may be ten completely separate lines. It is important to ensure that the lines are legible if the game is to work. The lines can be of any length but the game works best if they do not exceed one line of writing. (Sometimes it may be useful to stipulate a certain length or rhythm.)

The lines are then cut up and folded. These are collected in a hat or suitable container and mixed around. Each person will have put ten different lines into the pot, and each one then dips in and takes ten lines out.

This *is* a lucky dip, and it is possible that children will draw out one or two of their own lines but this does not matter. What follows is rather like a jigsaw puzzle as everyone moves the lines about and tries to create a poem from them. Tenses of verbs may be changed and odd link words may be omitted or added where necessary (e.g. prepositions, conjunctions). This can also be played with a variation which allows each person to add in two new lines wherever these would help the sense and run of the poem.

The value of this game is mainly to exercise the mind in playing with, and thinking about, words. It is fun to do and children enjoy the challenge it presents. Having to write ten lines quite quickly in the beginning is useful practice and often produces good lines which children may want to keep and work from later. Trying to make sense of ten random lines can also result in interesting phrases or groups of lines which, again, could be taken up later on. This can be a good way of showing that chance is one element in the writing of poetry, and the fortuitous combinations of unlikely or disparate thoughts and ideas which can create a memorable image and throw new light onto a subject. There are no new themes in poetry, all poems are really treating the same concerns of man – the art is to find the new angle, or different ways of saying the same thing.

Bran Tub

This is similar to Lucky Dip and might even use some of the lines written for that game. The Bran Tub is really an ideas pot and can be left around the classroom and used at any time. The children are asked to write a number of separate lines which are then cut up and collected in the pot. If they have a few isolated good lines in an otherwise mediocre poem they might like to put these in too. However, if a child is attached to his own line and feels possessive about it he must keep it for himself. The pot is now available for anyone to dip into and find an idea for a poem.

This time the children only take one line which attracts them and they use it somewhere in the poems they write. They should be allowed a little time to sift through until they find a line which fires their imagination, but with plenty to choose from this should not take too long. It may be that more than one child will use the same line – all lines should be returned to the tub. It may also be that once the line has served its purpose of setting the child writing, it may not appear in the poem at all. Children like the feeling that the writing stimulus comes from amongst themselves but if they have a pride in their work they will probably not want someone else's words in their own poems. It is also a well known fact that many people begin writing about one thing and find, as they proceed, that the poem is creating its own impetus and very often results in being about something totally different. The original stimulus was necessary but can then be discarded. It has tapped the imagination and set it loose to meander off on its own.

Mime the Rhyme

This game can be played in odd moments, or used specifically to accustom children to think of rhymes before writing some poems where rhyme will be used. It can also help those children who are not quite sure of true rhymes and seem to have some difficulty in hearing them.

A small group (perhaps four children) is sent out of the room. While outside, they think of a word, preferably one for which there are a number of rhymes. For example, they might choose the word 'bed'. They return into the room and tell the class that their word rhymes with, let us say, 'bread'. The class then has to guess the original word.

This is done by thinking of words that also rhyme with 'bread' and miming those words. Some of the words they might mime would be *dead, lead, red, fed, head, shed*, and so on. The small group watches and must identify the word being mimed. If it is not the original word they must say, 'No, it is not . . . ' (here they say the mimed word). If the group cannot guess the word being mimed it loses a point to the class. The group gains a point for every mime guessed correctly. This is continued until the group is forced to say, 'Yes, it is "bed".' If the word 'bed' were mimed as someone lying down to sleep, it is perfectly legitimate for a member of the group to say, 'No, it is not "sleepyhead",' even though it is fairly obvious that the mimer meant 'bed'. This is where ingenuity can come in. As long as the word rhymes, and could be said to represent the mime, it must be accepted and the class must think of another way to mime 'bed'.

This game gives children valuable practice in thinking of many different rhymes for a word instead of choosing the first one that comes to mind. If they are to use rhyme in their poetry it is essential that they use it properly. Too many poems are spoilt by bad rhyme. What a poem is trying to say is the most important thing and should not be lost through the use of ridiculous rhymes. Children will also become aware that some words have few rhymes and using them might result in forced writing which spoils the poem.

Rhyming Consequences

This is a game that can be played with children once they are used to using rhyme; they should probably have played Mime the Rhyme quite often before attempting this.

Each child has a piece of paper and something with which to write. Everyone writes a line that will begin a poem. These are passed round the circle so that each child has the line written by the person on his or her right (or left). The next step is for the children to write a second line which rhymes with, and follows on the sense of, the first line they have received. They then write a new (third) line continuing the subject but not rhyming, and fold the first two back out of sight. The papers are again passed on and, seeing only this new (third) line, the children must write a line that rhymes and follows on the sense of the line they have visible. These two are also folded back and a new (fifth) line is written, etc. This process continues until the poem is felt to be long enough – probably about twelve or fourteen lines, ending on a rhyme.

The fun comes when the poems are unfolded and read out. Points to emphasise before playing this game are that handwriting should be as clear as possible and end of line words should be chosen carefully to allow for someone else having to rhyme with them. There are very few words that have no rhymes, but there *are* some (what rhymes with 'secret'?), and also there are plenty of words that have perhaps only one or two rhymes, some of which children would be unlikely to know.

Person, Place, Weather, Time

I first heard of this game being used by the novelist and poet Russell Hoban and it has proved very successful on all levels, with both adults and children. It can give rise to poems or prose pieces and can be used simply as a game, or more often as a full session which can be repeated any number of times as the ingredients always change. No preparation is needed, spontaneity is all-important.

Choose four children; one will be *person*, the second, *place*, the third, *weather*, and the fourth, *time*. The first one is asked to think of a person, real or imaginary, in fact or in fiction. There must be a few details, perhaps concerning the age of the person, the sex, state of mind, or clothing. The second child thinks of a place, again with some details of description but excluding time and weather conditions. The third thinks of a type of weather and the fourth sets the time, perhaps the year, season and time of day. Each child thinks of these things quietly, without reference to any other, for a few minutes at the most. Then they each tell the class what they have imagined. The four elements combine to produce the bones of a story, albeit sometimes rather surreal.

Everyone then has ten to fifteen minutes *only* in which to write something. This may contain all the information given, or it may derive from only one part of what was said. It may, indeed, contain nothing that was mentioned but be about something that was sparked off by one of the things said. It is essential, however, that the time allowed for writing is limited. There are occasions when children should not be rushed and there are times when it is better to get something down quickly. Both practices should be encouraged as they open up different facets of the imagination. Interesting things can emerge from this exercise and children can always polish and organise their thoughts later if they have something they wish to work on.

When the time is up everyone reads out what has been written. It is fascinating for the whole class to hear what others have done. The pieces always vary so much and yet they originated from the same stimulus. The different styles, the various points that have been taken up and expanded upon, help to show how the same subject can be dealt with by different people, the wealth of possibilities that exists in the treatment of any one thing.

EXAMPLES
The four elements which gave rise to the following poems were – *Queen Victoria* at *Trafalgar Square* at *9.30 pm* in *1666* and it is *raining*. All the poems take as their starting points only one aspect of the original 'story'.

Nelson

The water is rippling gently,
The music begins.
My lions do not tire but guard me forever.
Here I stand reminding people of a war,
My only eye beginning to go blind,
My only arm breaking off,
My memory beginning to stick.
Kismet or kiss me? I don't know.
The words echo through my mind
Fading gently.

Jason Sewards

The Plague

The wooden house darkens in silence,
A red cough slowly becomes black,
Roses are laid across his grave
With a white cross waiting

Tony Reed

Drought

I am punishing the earth for its liking of the rain.
I shall make the earth rotate at my mercy.
I can do this
For I am the sun, hater of wetness,
Maker of light, radiator of the skies.

Zak Hall

9.30 pm 1666

The rattle of carts on the cobblestones,
The smoke rising from the chimneys,
Dogs barking at the horses.
Through an open window I see a man writing
His quill quivering as it scratches the paper,
The man writing his diary.
The flame flickers as all his thoughts
Of the day are recalled
And caged on the page.
His coded shorthand multiplies
As it eternally grows.
He strains his eyes in the candlelight.

Ben Owen

Trafalgar Square

My name is Nelson,
Admiral of the Navy,
Standing on the crow's nest looking out to sea.
Eternally crippled by a strait jacket of cement,
Writing my fixed bearings in the ship's log.
Up to the top! cried a pigeon,
What can you see?
I see no ships
But I see the smog.

Ben Owen

Picture Quotes

This game was described to me by Miss Anne Bourn Harvey as something she used to play at school. It is a game for children who have had more exposure to poetry than a beginner. It demands some shared knowledge of poems and is played as follows. Somebody thinks of a quotation and draws a picture of it on the board. Everyone else has to guess the quotation. Since no teacher would probably be encouraging children to write without also exposing them to reading and listening to poetry this game could be played with most classes. They could even try illustrating lines from their own poems which the rest of the class knew. The example that most amused me was of a girl who chalked a smudge on the board and then proceeded to rub it out. This was to illustrate 'Out, damned spot!'

Tall Stories

This is a game of invention and performance. Two teams are needed and both sides must use their imagination and vocabulary to invent the sort of exaggerated accounts of incidents that one can often hear over the public bar. It draws its inspiration from those people we all know who, when they tell a story, always make a performance out of it. Facts are readily twisted for dramatic effect and everything they tell you makes their lives sound interesting.

The children are asked to imagine that something has happened but they are not told what it is. Each child in one team then writes down a sentence or two beginning with the words, 'It was so funny I . . .' The members of the other team do the same but begin with the words, 'It was so awful I . . .' When they have finished both teams stand in a line facing each other and take it in turns, alternating team to team, to deliver their sentences. The result is usually very entertaining as it switches from mood to mood, each person trying to outdo the ones before.

EXAMPLE

Team 1   It was so funny it made Groucho Marx look like Margaret Thatcher.

Team 2   It was so awful I wished the ground had swallowed me up and not even spat out the bones.

Team 1   It was so funny even the birds were laughing so hard they fell out of the trees.

Team 2   It was so awful that Anne Boleyn rejoiced since she'd only had her head cut off.

Team 1   It was so funny that I laughed for a whole year and got into the Guinness Book of Records.

17

Team 2 It was so awful, I cried so much that they had to draw a new ocean on all the world maps.

And so it goes on.

101 Ways to Speak

This is not really a game at all, rather an exercise in vocabulary extension or thesaurus work, but it seems to belong in this chapter best. I include it as I think children enjoy doing it and it falls into the category of playing with words.

We made a very large chart and put a painted open mouth in the centre. The children and I together wrote down on the board all the words we could think of which meant 'speaking' in some way, e.g. utter, scream, shout, mumble, chatter, simper, whimper, declaim, gabble, grumble, say, interject, dispute, whisper. As the total rose we all decided to try to find 101 ways – which we did. In fact there were a few more but 101 sounded better so we stuck to that. Each child then took a number of the words to write out on pieces of card which were then stuck all over the chart. It was quick, easy and fun to do and the children were amazed at how many words they could find.

This encouraged us to try for 202 ways to move, but having become so involved in the whole exercise the children actually went on by themselves to find 303 ways. They searched their knowledge, 'tapped' parents at home and rummaged through dictionaries to come up with words. The sort of things that were included were sidle, shuffle, limp, dash, meander, saunter. These we also put onto a large chart with a running pin-man in the centre and the caption *303 Ways to Move*.

Playing with words in this way is an essential part of the back-up teaching of English and of writing in particular. Children enjoy new words and sounds and certainly improve their use of dictionaries and their spelling and vocabulary in a way that is more fun than some of the dry exercises offered in grammar books.

Other groups of words and wordplay that can be explored are spoonerisms, palindromes; words that spell another word backwards (e.g. drab and bard); words that are spelt the same but sound different (e.g. bow and bow; wind and wind); words that are spelt differently but sound the same (e.g. right, write, rite; cue, queue and Kew); rhyming compounds (e.g. huggermugger, helterskelter, humdrum, pellmell), and vowel change compounds (e.g. zigzag, dillydally, pitterpatter, singsong).

2 FROM EVERY ANGLE

One of the things we are teaching children through poetry is how to use their senses. It is too easy, and many children do it, to write about something in a superficial manner. Anyone can say that 'the flowers are pretty colours', or that a stone is 'an interesting shape'. These sort of observations are not special, they do not make anything 'come alive' or startle us by their originality. Television feeds us with constant pictures and sounds, occasionally drawing our attention to significant or interesting points, but hardly ever asking us to look properly for ourselves or describe our experience in words. As children grow older they begin to lose the infant's fascination with new sights, and it is necessary to make them look harder, use their minds and find fresh ways of describing what they see. So often it is details that make poems. Universal truths are more poignantly expressed by the small experience described in detail. The concrete images that symbolise the wider aspect of life are the things that we notice and remember.

Therefore, the old idea of presenting children with objects, or sending them out to look at a particular thing, has a very definite place in the teaching of poetry. Like any other exercise, of course, it should be used with discretion and not 'done to death'. In fact, almost all the exercises in this book are aimed at encouraging the children to think more deeply about their subject. This one merely highlights the necessity for using detailed concrete images.

The children must work hard to produce something which is good. It will take time and this should be allowed for. If you can read some good examples of the kind of thing you are after, and make it clear that it is new and original descriptions you expect, most children will respond and will experience that greater feeling of achievement that comes with producing something that is not just 'dashed off'. As teachers, we often expect too little and the children react accordingly. We all need to be pushed, enthused and encouraged before we necessarily work to our best ability. In time the children will want to do this for themselves, for their own satisfaction, but to begin with outside stimulation is needed.

EXAMPLES

The Stone

White as chalk
It glistens at me
Like glass when cut.
Its surface smooth,
In places rough
Where it has been chipped
And cut from a white sea-stone.
I feel it is alive.
After all the cold mantelpieces
And dusty shelves
It has been laid on
And all the careless hands
It has been dropped from
It is surely dead.
But no, it still glistens,
And its depths glow white
Like cats' eyes.
Yet if it is alive
How can it stay the same so long,
Chipped once, and only once
And no marks to show how old it is?
While I grow
I change my image
And will later die,
This stone will never die
And other hands will hold it as I do.

Diccon Alexander (YWW)

Paperweight

As I looked at it, I took it all in; the conical top, the imprisoned purple flower with the light shining through, the green colour flecked with brown that surrounded the flower and the tiny air bubbles trapped, all trapped inside the thick smooth glass. I picked it up, it was heavy, cold and hard. It was quite large and took up all my hand. I turned it slowly around. The petals were distorted and the green-brown surroundings seemed to bob like tiny waves one minute, then turn menacingly to protect the flower.

Facing it to the window I saw thousands of
tiny windows reflected onto the glass. I pulled
away lest the windows too would get trapped
inside the heavy-looking air. Startled by the
thought I held it close to my face. It smelt warm
and reminded me of pressing my nose against a
window in the pouring rain. Looking again I
saw my own face reflected. Shuddering I
replaced it in its spot on the mantelpiece and
looked out of the window at the sun bouncing
off the crazy paving.

Megan Trudell (YWW)

Meadows

The bull walked on the ready spread lawn,
He looked at his reflection in a small pool.
The wind blew the water and his face splintered.

Sheep stood grazing in the rising of the sun,
Hidden in trees lay a fox, his teeth burning,
Nearby cows watched the grass grow.

The cat watched the drenched fieldmice
Dart from shadow to light.
Fish slipped through weeds
Breathing bubbles greenly into the sky.

Melissa Cooke

A Thought in Lulworth Church

Midsummer
and the sky burns mellow in the light.
Golden and sweet roll the beaches,
glossy and warm.
Is a tear enough to quench the throat of time?
But the wind still hums through the dry chalk hills.
Such gossip blows round the old white fields.
Is a cry enough to deafen the ears of time?
I look through the leadlined windows
to see the wind singing in long white gowns
and the short sea-beaten bushes standing still
like pews in the dull summer breeze.

Miles Greene (YWW)

Daffodil

Yellow bells attached to green bell ropes,
A trumpet of pollinated notes.
Their starry shaped bonnets with curved edges
Hide their yellow faces.

Anna Cheifetz

3 CHALK OUTLINE

This idea was first suggested to me by the poet Kit Wright, who used it very successfully with a group of top primary children on an Arvon course (see Chapter 21, page 94, for a description of the Arvon Foundation). It uses the element of surprise and therefore needs to be set up carefully in advance of a lesson.

A place must be chosen with a large enough floorspace (or outdoors) to enable someone, preferably an adult, to lie down in an unnatural pose, as if he had fallen. I have done this myself and asked a colleague to chalk round the outline of my body on the floor. On one occasion this was done in a small room not much used in school, and first thing in the morning before the children arrived. I then took them to see it, having told them there had been a break-in and that the person had been taken by the police who had left the chalk outline on the floor. Some crime had perhaps been committed? However, the children do not have to think on these lines at all. The outline of the person is merely a different stimulus for writing and they should be encouraged to approach their poems in any way they choose.

It perhaps offers more scope if the outline is drawn on the classroom floor under a carpet, if you have one. At the appropriate time you can roll back the carpet to show what you had found, to your surprise, that morning. The children should try to forget they are in a classroom and just stare at the chalk figure. They should ask themselves how it might have arrived on the floor, who it was, what story lies behind it? With the right sort of discussion, which leads them away from the present into the imagination, the resulting poems can be quite astounding. An extension of this could be to present the children with pictures of the many fascinating chalk figures which can be seen around the countryside, or better still, if possible, take them to see one or two. Those who live in the West Country are luckier in this respect as that is where most of these figures can be seen. Some of the most famous of these figures are the Uffington, Osmington, Westbury and Pewsey Horses, the Cerne Abbas Giant, the Wilmington Man and the Whipsnade Lion.

EXAMPLES

The Strange Native

At number 27 Harfude Street
A native lived.
He came from South America.
He had taken a hobby up.
Discarding his native dance
He danced the way of Africa.
The swerving movement left no time for air.
He had a record of Ipi Tombi.

Christina Young

No Way of Knowing

It lay there, mangled and twisted, like a snake
digesting. As soon as the story was told, that
Peter Shortly had slipped into the river and had
been churned into pulp and flesh, sparkling like
flamboyant blood, the fireplaces were being
used, and his family knew before he got to the
third house. His wife, mother and two sons
came out crying.
   Now he lies there without knowing what his
future will be. He hopes a good one but it may
be as bad as a frog's life, or it may be a golden
king for the children of Bob Wood.

Roddy Mattinson

(Note: The above piece draws on local superstition in the area
around Lumb Bank, Yorkshire, where there is supposed to be a
ghost in Bob Wood. The 'fireplaces' refers to the custom in Heptonstall of banging on the fireplaces down a row of houses to pass
messages quickly if something was happening. This would bring
people to their doors. This information was given to the children
by folk singer, Bob Pegg, who was resident oral traditionist at the
Arvon Foundation for a few years.)

The Strange Case of Inspector Welsh

'Inspector Welsh' was going
from the kitchen to the dining room
when a cricket ball flew through the window

and hit him right on the temple
which killed him immediately.
His body was taken away
and a chalk outline drawn.

All this happened
and the sausages sat through it all,
eye-witnesses that didn't say anything.

Susan O'Dell

The Chalk Horse

On a giant green blackboard
Is a horse
Drawn by a million teachers
With white dusty chalk.
A thousand pupils have come to admire it,
To stand on the gritty figure
Or to admire from afar
Their teachers' handiwork.
Historians attach legends and battles to it,
Great kings defeated,
Human sacrifices burnt on it,
Iron Age tribes performing ancient rituals,
Bonfires were lit on it,
Dragons were fought, people were killed . . .

Laura Bacharach (YWW)

The Dragon's Flight

I stop out of breath and rest,
Then continuing I trudge up the hillsides,
One after the other.
The sun comes out, over the wild deserted hills.
It is a dragon that is resting on the hillside,
It is a dragon,
I can feel it
Winging through the sky on the back of the clouds.
The sight before me dazzles my eyes,
It is there, the dragon,
White, huge, beautiful.
The dragon moves,
Its hot breath stirs my hair.
It starts to tramp across the hill

Its white chalked body following obediently.
The head looks up to the rushing clouds.
Its legs poise, white wings unfurl,
Gently its body lifts off the hill.

Nadya Kassam (YWW)

4 ANIMALS

Children always like animals, whether it be domestic pets or the more exotic wild creatures of the world. They will frequently write about them as well as thoroughly enjoying the books they read with animal characters. Books such as *Tarka the Otter*, *Watership Down*, *The Mouse and his Child* will always have a devoted following. This can be a subject which presents pitfalls however. Either they write stories and poems anthropomorphising the animals in often a banal way, or the poems are superficial in their observation of animals and their behaviour. Wild animals too often 'pounce on their prey' without any clear picture being given of what the 'prey' might be. 'Prey' is a word that seems to appeal so much to children that, if you are not careful, it occurs time and time again. It has become one of my *bêtes noires*, as it were, and belongs to the 'woolly' abstract language that does poetry such a disservice. 'Dripping jaws', 'blood' and 'death' also tend to occur with monotony in the 'prey' poems and we have all, no doubt read too many of them in our lifetime.

Nevertheless, animals are a subject that will always fascinate children and if we are going to encourage better writing we must make sure that the same detailed approach is followed as in other exercises. We should not allow our sentimentality towards animals to affect our judgement of the poems.

One of the best ways to assist the children is to arrange for them actually to study a real live animal, either in the countryside, the classroom or the zoo, so that they can describe it in proper detail. Alternatively, or as well, they can find a picture to have in front of them while they work. They can be encouraged to read up about the animal in order to be able to use interesting facts which will help the authenticity of their writing. All these details will ensure that the poems are more successful than those written entirely from imagination. It means they must use their senses more and find ways of describing the animals which are more vivid, perhaps involving the use of metaphor and simile. A storyline can be interwoven in the poem but the whole thing will start with the concrete image.

There are many good examples of famous animal poems which can be read to the children to help encourage them to be more specific in their observation. Notable amongst these are some

27

poems by Ted Hughes, e.g. 'Pike', 'The Jaguar', 'A March Calf', 'Swifts', and there are countless other examples by different poets to be found in most anthologies. It is also very worthwhile to look through individual volumes of poetry to find poems which are not generally anthologised. There are some marvellous discoveries to be made which are all too often overlooked. Anthologies, of course, are most useful in schools but unfortunately one frequently gains the impression that the editors have only read other anthologies and the same poems occur time and time again.

EXAMPLES

The Bullock

Your neck like an old empty sack,
Hooves like polished wood,
Your fur stuck together by mud.
Every time you chew
Your whole bottom lip moves back and forth.
You fill the air with your repeated breath,
You come forward inquisitive,
You stare at me.

Pippa Monjardino

The Welsh Mountain Pony

The small head of the Welsh pony
Drops to pluck the coarse heather on the mountain side,
Like a miniature Arab he prances and sidles.
He flicks his pure white tail to and fro,
Whilst the flies irritate his hindquarters.
His hooves are like pebbles on a beach
Tattooing a steady pace.
His mane is like watered silk
As it flows in the wind.
His legs, small but fast-moving,
Beat out a canter into the horizon.

Rebecca Luff

The Cobra

His marks are honeycomb
His eyes are like flying saucers,
His ribs stretch like elastic bands.

The curled teeth shining and ready for a victim.
His back patterns are stars in the moonlight.

Sharon Purves

Sheep

Standing erect against aged wind
Grazing on familiar grass,
Raises its head as if woken from sleep.
Two pointed ears stick out of that meek head,
Only fields are known to him.
Never venturing far, stopped by a brambled boundary,
The feel of life's countdown slowing its stride.

John Nathan

House Fly

I am sworn at and unpraised. My eyes are like
deep chocolate pools. I love to wallow in sugar
for that makes me live longer. My wings are
transparent and my chest is grey but the rest of
me is a type of gloss and soot black. I swerve and
dive and complete many irregular triangles.

Laurence Hopkinson

The Vulture

A bald old man with old fashioned ruffs, his
suit looks like an old black flag fluttering in the
wind. He is like a scarecrow, a raggedy tramp,
he looks out of place in his many habitats. His
feet are smooth yet bumpy. You can't see his
fingers until he flies, then he has many. On the
ground he looks like a solemn undertaker.

David Travers

Unicorn

A colour so difficult to describe. Perhaps the
colour of the foam in the sea – so white, but yet
so dark. A single horn of a twisting tapering
design set neatly in the middle of the forehead.
Belonging to this horn are magical powers such

as it can cure any disease or wound.

The deep brown eyes give off the image of the forest in which the unicorn lives. They live alone in a forest that never grows old, with pools so clear they can see themselves, for knowing they are the most beautiful they are a little vain.

The hooves are cloven and give the unicorn such a graceful movement that no other animal has except deer in shy imitation and goats in dancing mockery.

Unicorns are immortal and no place is ever more enchanted than where one has been born.

Andy Henry

5 CHARACTERS FROM LITERATURE

One of the accusations sometimes levelled at poetry and prose writing is that it too often tends to feed on itself, to write about writing and writers. But there are a number of examples where this has been highly successful, among them are 'Mastering the Craft' by Vernon Scannell, 'The Thought-Fox' by Ted Hughes and 'The Maker' by R. S. Thomas, and these show that this area is worth exploring.

A practice that many teachers follow in class is to ask children to write reviews of books they have read. I suspect this is often simply to check that a child has read the book properly, but it also provides practice in critical appreciation and a store of reviews for other children to read, and possibly to encourage them in their choice of what to read next. There is nothing like the seal of approval from one of your peers; it often carries more weight than a mere teacher's suggestion.

Occasionally, however, it may be good to suggest that poems should be written about a book or a character in it. This is different from a review, and gives the opportunity for a more creative appreciation as opposed to the often regurgitated form of the story which can be accomplished with little work and less satisfaction, or can seem just a chore to children who are eager to move on to their next book.

But an exercise like this can also be done as a writing lesson in itself without reference to the current reading book of each child. They are simply asked to choose a character from fiction and write a poem about him or her, trying to include the details which will make this character recognisable to others. Any form can be used, although all the examples here are acrostics which can be an aid to the children's writing. The name of the character is spelt out in the first letters of each line.

EXAMPLES

B lack as night he stands
L ike fire burning the wind.
A future with a cover,
C ompanions, friends, enemies,
K indness and unkindness too.

B eauty like a bird in the wind.
E mptiness, a blank page.
A very merry friend,
U nhappiness and happiness.
T ime and time fly,
Y ears until the end.

Katy Miles

D reaming of what lies ahead in London,
I nterested but sad to depart from his home town.
C oming to see what fortune there is to find,
K illing his heart at the thought of leaving.

W ondering which way to turn.
H eading for a town paved with gold.
I s it going to be worth it,
T his journey to a far off place?
T empted to buy a cat for companionship.
I ntervals before carrying on the heavy pace.
N o-one there to ask any questions,
G asping for breath,
T he cat whimpering for some milk,
O bserving the bells that ring out merrily,
N ew-fangled buildings.

Michele Collins

S tunned by the bare body of a rose
L eaving torn remains,
E nding a quiet sleep of piercing silence
E yes closed like a book, not to be opened till opened.
P anes of sleep cover the castle,
I n the hall people stand still – frozen time –
N ot able to eat the last chocolate.
G reat bushes like a web surround the castle.

B reathing, alive, but her face does not change.
E arly dust collects, settles on everything.
A ll noise is stopped, motion unknown.
U p the stone stairs that spiral round,
T rickles of blood fall from the needle's destination,
Y awning mouths open as a lip touches a cheek.

Pippa Monjardino

F lying through the air
L ike a bird.
A s clean as a swallow
S miling down onto the land
H igh flying – it looks grand.

G ordon flies through the sky in his
O bject, ripping the air like pulling
R oots out of a plant.
D oes Flash get killed?
O r does he defeat the enemy?
N ow use your imagination.

Zaki Standing

P addington's imagination was to his own
    disadvantage,
A lways getting himself into trouble,
D aily entrusting himself into the hands of fate.
D oomed by his will to help.
I n Windsor Gardens things are never quiet.
N ose tingling at the thought of another adventure,
G rossly indulged in eating a sandwich,
T atty old hat upon his head,
O range marmalade shines on his snout.
N ever knows what will happen next.

Ben Owen

6 STARING

We have all, no doubt, experienced the feeling of staring at something for a long time – flames, water, clouds – and know the kind of meandering thoughts this provokes as well as the succession of pictures conjured up by the shapes and movement, given form in our imagination. As children we would often play the game of seeing pictures in the open fire. A poem by Ted Walker, 'Clouds', which can be found in his book *The Solitaries* (Jonathan Cape), deals with this kind of experience.

It can be used with great success as an exercise in writing for the children. The idea is to stare at something for a long time and to jot down all the pictures you begin to see. The sort of things which lend themselves to this are a blank area of wall, a single brick, a puddle, a piece of bark, a square of earth or grass or playground, the palm of a hand, a post or railings, a gate, looking through a marble to the light, a cloud, a dark corner, and so the list can go on. If you stare long enough your imagination begins to take over and a succession of thoughts and pictures emerge which should be written down immediately. These impressions form notes which can be worked on to produce poems. It is a simple exercise, easy to organise, but can lead to fascinating results particularly when children are used to writing and can draw the threads together so that they say even more than a straight description. This gives practice in finding other ways to describe something, which leads naturally into the use of metaphor, an important technique in the writing of poetry. However, in the early stages with a class the purpose of opening up the imaginative processes of the mind makes this an exercise of great value.

EXAMPLES

Railings

The sea rippling on a cool day,
Kings and queens standing in a row,
Pieces of string, some tied loose, some tight,
And a head of hair.
Rows of hills reflected in water,
Faces staring at each other
And a row of spears,

Nine pieces of paper, each with a tear,
A line of washing hanging to dry.

Helen Alexander

Seeing

I see thickets where deer run and hide,
I see the ocean with its snatching tide,
I see the field where hero Harold died,
I see my death bride.

I see Cranmer flame in pain,
I see the ark awash in biblical rain,
I see the chalk stallion's silver mane,
I follow thought's long and winding lane.

Nicholus Tomkins

Stone

Great Britain,
A group of magpies
Screaming for ancient coins.
Dirty beach,
An old stone ruin.
An owl sees his future.

Joanna Cooper

The Image in the Brick

In the darkness of the brick
I see a steep rocky cliff with one dull grey colour.
I also see ghostly objects like stiff witches,
Outlines of blurry skulls with no bones
And gorillas with no eyes.
I can see rocky objects,
Meteorites falling from the sky
Making volcanoes which dry up
To make a mountain with a steep hill,
Almost a cliff, but without rock.

Pawel Gorajewski

7 MOONSHINE

I remember the day the Americans first landed on the moon. I remember watching, with mild interest, the dreamlike pictures on a black and white television set as the astronauts disturbed the dust of the Mare Tranquillitatis. I know, because I was told, that it was a 'giant leap for mankind' and yet I could not then, nor since, raise the same enthusiasm I still feel for the old-fashioned romantic and mystical moon. For me there are at least four moons: the space reality with its echoes in science fiction, fascinating in a way with its arid lunar landscapes and uninhabited desolation; the Diana of literature and legend; the heavenly body I see in all its phases over a silvered countryside, a natural beauty attended by intriguing superstition; and a fourth which exists purely in my imagination, arising from the wonderful poetic names given to the different areas by the astronomer, Hevelius, who first catalogued his discoveries from earth. I am struck by the fact that a scientist should have chosen such melodious names, and, as it turns out, such inappropriate ones. Sad to say, subsequent astronomers who made more discoveries through their telescopes were not as inventive.

However, we can still dream and the names which have survived can provide a marvellous list of possibilities for writing. Such places as the Sea of Tranquillity, the Lake of Dreams, the Ocean of Storms, the Bay of Rainbows and the Sea of Nectar can allow children to create a fantasy moon which can be just as real, and even enhanced in a curious way by the complete incompatibility of the names with the reality. The very dust and dryness of the moon's surface cries out for water which our imagination can provide.

The children can be asked to find the names of interest from a modern atlas, which usually contains a map of the moon, and these can be written on the board, or the teacher can just write the list out. Some discussion will probably be useful along the lines I have been following above. The children must be able to free themselves from the reality and concentrate on creating their own dreams which they can be encouraged to approach from any angle they like. They just choose one of the names to act as the title and stimulus for a poem. Since the names were originally in Latin, and as such can sound even more magical and exciting, it is a good idea to allow the choice of the original or the translation. Children enjoy new words, particularly when they have a good ring to them, and will love to hear the Latin rolling off their tongues.

Mare Imbrium	–	Sea of Rains
Mare Nubium	–	Sea of Clouds
Mare Crisium	–	Sea of Crises
Mare Humorum	–	Sea of Moisture
Mare Nectaris	–	Sea of Nectar
Mare Serenitatis	–	Sea of Serenity
Mare Tranquillitatis	–	Sea of Tranquillity
Mare Vaporum	–	Sea of Vapours
Mare Fecunditatis	–	Sea of Fertility
Mare Frigoris	–	Sea of Cold
Mare Marginis	–	Border Sea
Mare Cognitum	–	Known Sea
Sinus Iridium	–	Bay of Rainbows
Sinus Aestuum	–	Seething Bay
Sinus Roris	–	Bay of Dew
Sinus Medii	–	Central Bay
Lacus Somniorum	–	Lake of Dreams
Lacus Mortis	–	Lake of Death
Oceanus Procellarum	–	Ocean of Storms

It is only fair to say that I do not think the following poems are as successful as I might have hoped. The fault very probably lies with me. I feel that this aspect of the moon may not have appealed to the children as much as it did to me, or I may not have put it across as well as possible. However, there are always times when something does not seem to work, but this does not always mean that the idea is wrong. Another group of children might respond better, or I might present the idea better. It is worth persisting and not giving up too easily. At the same time we should not be afraid to admit defeat occasionally.

EXAMPLES

Lake of Dreams

Go to the Lake of Dreams
And soak an eagle's head in the waters.
Write the dream you wish in the sand
Using the bird's beak.

Take that sand and throw it in the Lake
Then jump in yourself.
You will fall into softness to land on the bottom
Where you will dream,
Dream recurring thoughts
Spilling out of the lip of your mind.

Josh Hillman

Lacus Somniorum

Green mist-like waters,
Brightly coloured fish swim by.
Green waters rush past,
My head lifts.
I lay myself down on the dry reed bed
And dream in my thoughts
That I work by Rowpool
And drift under the trees of Radnor Forest.
I dream of the fire in the forest,
How my dad went to fight it,
How it made my dad insure Hill House
In the heart of Radnor Forest
By Bleddfa village
Where the last wolf in Wales was shot.

Katy Miles

Central Bay

Central Bay is a deserted place
Untouched by hands of the human race,
Civilisation was never allowed,
Just rain and mist and maybe a cloud.
The nearby spaceman hidden in his layer
Still and scared he whispers a prayer.

Charles De' Ath

The Bay of Rainbows

Sparkling above, the almighty moon,
Never to rise, never to set,
Always to fascinate.
Lingering over the deep wishing well

That lies empty and abandoned
For little green men to play in.

Jason Sewards

Sea of Nectar

A pot of honey poisons the water with sweetness,
It sinks.
A flower is thrown in,
The bee has no time to escape.
The sweet smell lingers,
Dew settles on the water.

Pippa Monjardino

8 GIFTS

When a child is born it is customary for relatives and friends to bring presents for the newborn baby, and when it is christened the godparents usually give a gift. When Jesus was born, the Bible tells us the three Wise Men brought gifts of gold, frankincense and myrrh while according to legend the shepherds gave a lamb. In fairy stories there are similar tales, notably in the Sleeping Beauty, of gifts being wished upon a child. In the one case it is three wise men and in others it is three wise women (or witches as they were sometimes known in past times). I believe it was also the custom among Red Indians to grant the new baby certain attributes and fortunes along with its special name.

All this led into an idea for poems which the children might write. And the idea is simply to write poems, possibly conceived as lullabies, which offer gifts which the children would like to give to a newborn child, whether they are within the bounds of possibility or not. This idea can be used as a new angle for Christmas poems or can be written for an imaginary baby. The poem can also be written for a particular baby – perhaps a new brother or sister – or can be given an historical setting which would enable the writer to bring in details of fact or legend as has been done with the 'Viking Cradle Song' in the examples below.

EXAMPLES

Lullaby for Christ

I have brought you a fox so you will have knowledge,
I have brought you a wolf so you will have courage,
I have brought you a hare so you will be swift
But your heart will be weak and sometimes fail you.
Now I bring you myrrh, I bring you gold,
I bring you wise men with stories to be told
I have brought you frankincense with a sweet smell,
I have brought you followers who wish you well.
You will have no temper, you will have no wrath,
And you will die an heroic death.

Ben Owen

Viking Cradle Song

Hush, child, hush,
No need to cry,
For you will be the strongest of them all.
Stronger than Thor and his mighty hammer,
And do good and bad,
But you will have no love to give.

Hush, child, hush,
For Ymir the Ice Giant
Has asked for your hand in marriage.
There you shall dwell in twelve years' time.
But beware, Ymir will steal your love
And let the dwarfs change it into hate for Asgard.

Hush, child, hush,
For you will become goddess of all women.
Live to be healthy, grow to love,
Live till Ragnar's day.
See the world from Odin's cliff of powers.

Hush, child, hush,
For Jormungand
Has offered to let you round the world
Upon his back,
If you can steal the Brisingamen
And let him have a glimpse of it.

Hush, child, hush,
For one of its beads
Is a torch of the world
And of Ragnar's day.
Steal back the torch
And Odin will give you
A drop of the Mead of Inspiration.

Melissa Cooke

Lullaby

I bring you sea so that you can create
Fish and underwater mammals.
You will go on a voyage
And see new lands and natives.

You have a fault in your right arm
And will cast away the death from it.
You will be eternal, eternal,
Eternal, eternal, eternal.

Your life has begun but has far to go.
The baby will be gentle and prudent.
I've brought you a world so you may live in it.
You shall be eternal, eternal,
Eternal, eternal, eternal.

The world is big, make use of it,
The ocean is wide, sail in it
You shall become a poet,
I give you paper, scar it.
You shall be eternal, eternal,
Eternal, eternal, eternal.

Karen Bounds

Different Doubles

Girl Your face will resemble half
Of the first flower in Spring.
You shall be as clever as an owl is not,
You will be clumsy as an owl is not,
You will be impatient as the moon is
While waiting to rise.

Boy Your face will resemble the other half
Of the first flower in Spring.
You shall be as fast as a cat being chased by a dog.
You will be forgetful as a man taking honey from
      bees,
And as slow at thinking as you will be fast.

Pippa Monjardino

9 THE MAKING OF . . .

This idea had its starting point in a poem called 'The Making of the Drum' by Edward Brathwaite which can be found in *Other Worlds* (The English Project, Stage One). This led to thinking about the making of other objects. A craftsman, a maker, essentially needs three things: an idea of what to make; the materials with which to make it; and the tools for the job. When making something in words the same rules can be applied – the materials will be mainly nouns and adjectives, and the tools will be verbs.

Once you have an idea, perhaps something you could not normally make, one way to begin is to compile a list of phrases (nouns and adjectives) to be used as the materials (often including things you could not really use), for example, 'the undertow of the treacherous tide' or 'the crackle of static'. Each phrase is chosen to illustrate a quality of the object. The verbs are the tools that mould and shape, so a list of interesting ones can be made, for example, lever, tilt, or skim. All that now remains is to use the tools to shape the materials, to put the ideas together using the verbs and create the original artefact.

EXAMPLES

The Making of the Tiger

One chip and another
As the line of his back
Begins to take shape,
The smooth curve
The gentle slope.
Another chip, and one more,
An ear begins to form,
The small hollow
With every detail
Comes to life.
The face and the staring eye
Seem to be alone,
Not with the body
The staring eye,
Not with the body

The motionless face,
The harsh silence.
The smooth stomach line
The graceful sloping curve
That glides to form the perfect shape.
A leg and a foot form in oak
As claws are cut
Like blades from a penknife.
The shape of the leg
The bend of the knee
Perfect to every precise detail.
As sandpaper smooths its body
And he breathes his breath into the form,
The great carver's work is done.

Nadya Kassam (YWW)

The Making of a City

The making of a city,
A huge city,
In the middle of a large space of land.
They knew it would take time,
They must not hurry or it would be ruined,
They must not take time
Or it would never be finished,
They must do it steadily, very steadily.
The bricks must be made out of huge pieces of rock,
The tools cut out of metals and wood.
Holes must be dug to make this city.
It will take years of hard work.

They must build fences pleased with their
    surroundings,
Dustbins annoyed with their uses,
Lampposts filled with joy at being able to see
    everything.
There will be parks of happiness,
Bricks filled with death,
Windows open to the sunshine,
Pavements filled with pain,
Trees that have the feeling of freedom
And branches happy with hope.

Lydia Masseron

The Making of a Grave

The rock is levered out of its home,
Scrambling woodlice roll into balls,
In the van it longs for freedom.

A silent scream echoes through the room
As the chisel stabs.
The distant chomping of a spade can be heard
Where the man with the measurer stands.

Charles De' Ath

The Making of a Redwood Tree

Come fire and burn open the cone,
Come wind and blow the seeds in all directions.
Come ash and make a bed for the newborn seeds.
Come rain, come sun, give water and heat,
Come time and wait for the seedling to appear,
Come buds and decorate with leaves.
Come birds and populate the tree,
Come birds and build a nest,
Come, eggs, hatch
For I feel dead without you.

Ben Owen

The Making of a Picture

To make a picture go into a wood.
Find a stream without a current
And cut a slice of water which will be paper.

To make a picture you must have tools.
Dig down and find a treasure chest,
Maybe it will have a paintbrush.

To make a picture you must have paint.
Sketch a ladder up to the skies
And cut some yellow off the sun,
Green from the treetops and blue from the sky.

To paint the picture collect a tree,
Some grass and a cat, iron them flat,
Stick them on and paint them over
In all the colours of a century.

John Nathan

10 OMENS

Superstitions thrive on people's susceptible imaginations and whether we are inclined to believe them or not, we all probably experience a twinge of foreboding if we spill the salt or look at a new moon through glass. Many of the superstitions have their origins in history or common sense, e.g. crossed knives usually did mean a quarrel when swords were still in use, and walking under a ladder may result in a tin of paint falling on your head. But many of them seem to have no basis in reality and can be flouted with no apparent consequent misfortune or good luck.

However, they do present a rich store of ideas which can be exploited by the writer and can help to build up a powerful atmosphere in a poem. The idea of sitting down to a meal with an extra place laid, for the visitor who might come, has always fascinated me, and the breaking of a mirror with its legendary seven years' bad luck can provide an immediate response from that part of our imagination that delves deep into fantasy. A useful poem that relies to some extent on superstition is 'Flannan Isle' by Wilfred Wilson Gibson.

Children are interested in this subject and enjoy writing about it. A whole class can spend a lesson just talking about various superstitions and old wives' tales which they know and discussing the value of them. Do they seem to make good sense and what might be their origins? Do they link up in any way with other beliefs? For example, throwing salt over your *left* shoulder with the *right* hand is supposedly good triumphing over evil, the salt thrown in the Devil's eyes. This can be associated with the story of Christ being tempted in the wilderness by the Devil traditionally looking over his shoulder, and gives substance to our use of the Latin word *sinister* (meaning 'left').

The children can then be asked to take a superstition and use it as a starting point for a poem. Alternatively, they can be encouraged, after a discussion, to create their own superstitions and enlarge on them in their writing. This is 'tapping' their interest in the magical or inexplicable element of belief which co-exists with rational thinking and can be worked into 'real' situations to give them more point and 'edge'.

EXAMPLES
Black Holly

Black evil pricks my earthly skin,
A sample for the underworld.
The days argue with each other
As I wait for my escort.
I lie on the cross of uncertainty
My life too short but death made it long.
I cherish each intake of earthly breath.
Black holly will be laid on my grave.

Hedy-anne Goodman

The Swans

The river runs red with the blood of many men.
The white trio with stuck out necks
Abandon the water to fly their death flight.
The trees are bare, the heavens dark,
There is no sound from the once singing lark.

Nicholas Tomkins

A Life Story

The first year
A slightly longer blade of grass –
Death under a knife.

The second year
The garden tree snapped –
I shall collapse.

The third year
A crack in the earth.
No coffin for my long sleep.

The fourth year
A crazy paving path.
A shattered gravestone for no-one to remember me.

The fifth year
The old man died.
My heart shall weaken.

The sixth year
I see a black-chested robin,
He came from the Devil's crucifixion.

The seventh year
A black cat crossed my path.
I wished for the curse to break.

Zak Hall

A Week of Strange Cats

On Monday a mischievous white cat followed me home
To be stroked and tickled.

On Tuesday I saw two kittens scrounging in a dustbin
And fighting over a dead fish.

On Wednesday three wild cats ate food out of my hand
Then vanished when it was gone.

On Thursday a tom cat killed four butterflies
And left them on the lawn.

On Friday five friendly cats spat at me
And arched their backs until their ribs ached.

On Saturday I heard six shy cats
Singing songs of sorrow.

On Sunday my cat died,
(Of scarlet fever).

Lydia Masseron

11 LAST WILL AND TESTAMENT

It is a fact that children frequently write about death, whether of animals or people, and this can often disturb some adults. A preoccupation with death would, naturally, give one cause to worry if it were overriding. But, generally this is not so and I believe that those adults who say that children should be writing about 'beautiful' and 'wonderful' things only are merely displaying their own inability to consider the fact of death and usually their ignorance of poetry. It is often these people, it seems to me, who tend to encourage children to read and write the harmless, often pointless, doggerel which passes for poetry in some anthologies and contains nothing of the craft, intelligence and exciting use of language we should be expecting from the children's work. One of the aspects of serious poetry which I look for and admire is its ability to disturb readers from everyday complacency and set them thinking about something in a way they never have before.

Children are quite fascinated with the subject of death and as yet have little or no experience of the absolute horrors which can come with age. They are upset if a relative or pet dies, of course, and it can be a marvellous release to be able to write about it. This applies to adults as well although they do not use this release enough. It is good to let children ask their questions and talk about death – it is a healthy curiosity.

The idea of writing a last will and testament is an attempt to bring in an almost positive side to this subject, and to make the children think of the joys of life which they might wish to leave to someone. This will is not meant to be a list of possessions in the material sense – that side of things can be rather morbid. It is, instead, to be a catalogue of things bequeathed which you could not normally leave to anyone. It will contain qualities of humanity, feelings and emotions, health and happiness – all the things you would want to wish for someone if you had the ability and chance. There is also scope for leaving things for the improvement of, say, someone you perhaps dislike – the corrective kind of will. The children will learn something about themselves doing this exercise – what things do they consider important and of value? – and will be looking at life and relationships in a way that should probe beneath the superficial layers, as long as they are honest with themselves.

EXAMPLES

Death Will

I have scrutinised my friends to write my death wishes.
My brother will receive my energy
Which I do not wish to keep.
With it I bestow my scorched reputation,
With this I have sighed too much.
To my sister I render my slumberous imagination
Which is of little use with its many a flaw.
To my father, my greatest love, I leave my life
As a memory that I hope will live with him.
I leave my joys and emotions
For him to find pleasure
As I did.

John Nathan

Last Wish

To you I grant a heart
For it is you who truly needs one.
I leave to you understanding
For though you seem to know it all
You are totally devoid of knowledge.
I take away from you the power to worship
For you seem not to want it.
I give you humility,
Practise having it in your possession.

Hedy-anne Goodman

Last Thoughts

My last ten minutes are given to you
In writing this will.
The last day of battle
And the French are ten thousand strong.
I have not long to live.
To my wife I give
All the flowers in a hundred acres
And my blessings go with all of them.
To our only son

I leave a choir of nightingales
Conducted at your command.
But to the enemy I am fighting
I leave the darkness of a hundred generations
And the Devil's curse.
Now I must leave for the pounding of hooves
Are drumming in my ears
And the roar of the cannon
And the shouts of the soldiers
Are ringing through my head.

Ben Owen

Last Thoughts

I grant a rib cage to the otter
Who has felt lead many a time.
The rib cage is as strong as a heart.
A bullet would not harm his confidence and trust.
I give a fish wisdom
For the fish has felt the hook
In his mouth many a time.
I hope it will not feel the pain again.

Zaki Standing

12 SHIP IN THE BOTTLE

I have always been interested in ships in bottles, ever since my father made one when I was young. The obvious fascination is firstly how the ship could be made to go through the narrow bottle neck. It appears to be a case of doing the impossible, and, even though I now know how it is done, I am still able to suspend disbelief and marvel at the phenomenon of a ship in full sail filling a bottle where reason says it should not be.

This is no less fascinating for children today. There is something magical and intriguing here which, I have found, attracts all children and has consistently given rise to remarkable pieces of writing. The discussion which precedes the writing might concentrate on the following aspects.

Who made the ship in the bottle and why? What kind of ship is it? How has it been made? All these things are to do with the 'outside' qualities which may interest some children and allow them to create a character and introduce historical detail to add substance to the poem. For me, it is the 'inside' possibilities that capture the imagination. To suppose that I could shrink myself in some way, like Alice, and enter through the neck of the bottle with the ship is an exercise of the mind which I find very satisfying. There is the element of exploration and yet what you find is completely yours – you are free to imagine what you want. As I am a tall person perhaps it is a need to crawl away into small corners, to be able to curl up in tiny spaces, to be on the inside.

But it works for children too. The genie in the bottle has always been a popular element in stories and Alice's experiences in Wonderland would seem to be relevant too. Children enjoy the idea of putting themselves into the bottle and imagining what it would be like on the ship. This ship goes nowhere, it is stuck in time and place with sails fully rigged and never a breath of wind to fill them. The sea is static, usually highly coloured in tones of cobalt and green with crests of white on the rough still waves. The sky is immediately the curve of the glass and the horizon is distorted by reflections that change. What would it be like to be a crew member of this ship, to be a tiny figure stuck into position with a specific job to do and yet no way of carrying it out? How would the captain of such a ship feel? Would commands echo out through the staleness of the trapped air with no-one able to obey them? Would the sailors long for a storm in order to be active, or would they rather reach land and go on leave? Possibly there is something ignobling in being trained and equipped for sailing and yet captured and 'pirated' away to a drawing room table or a museum case only to be stared at and conveniently carried from place to place. There is also the romantic air of 'tall ships' and 'before the mast' and the taste and sound of the sea – putting your ear to an empty bottle has the same effect as listening to a shell. Perhaps you can imagine that things *do* happen inside the bottle unnoticed by the world outside.

There are numerous angles the children can take by just looking and thinking. It is not absolutely necessary to have an actual ship in a bottle to show them – I never have – or, indeed, to have a picture of one. It could be useful, of course, and it is true to say that in most cases it is better to have something 'concrete' on which to base observations. Poems tend, as a general rule, to be more interesting and arresting the more specific they are. However, this must be judged according to the children you are dealing with and the subject they are being given. In this particular case, if the children are used to concentrating their imaginations, a good discussion can provide the details in such a way that each child has his or her own 'concrete' picture in mind which will be different from that of others. This will ensure that the poems are more individual and not so many reproductions of the same thing, which is to be avoided where possible.

EXAMPLES

Ship in a Bottle

Picture behind glass.
This life, now death,
This morning, now evening,
These years, just hell turned to stone.
I call to the helmsman,
I call to the captain,
I call to my god –
Sorry, their god.
He cannot see me,
For the child who sailed me
Through and around
The childish battles in his mind
Brought me to this steady mousetrap in his room.

I know I am not a sailor.
He, by my posed working hand, is not the captain,
That mindless man is not the helmsman
And they are not the crew.
We are behind the window of a craftsman's mind,
Strays from God's working hands in the sky.

Miles Greene

Ship in a Bottle

Floating on an aimless current,
A constant reminder that we'll never reach port.
Hope in a bottle is not easy to find
And happiness was lost in a storm.

Matthew Festenstein

Ship in the Bottle

It's not the real sea,
All I float in is wax.
I hear the water rushing up against my hull
But it's just echoes.
The sky is blotted out prematurely
By fingers that touch me,
Not clouds but people's hands.
Man made me small
So I would not look down on him.
My sails yearn to touch the wind
But the wind passes over me.

Orson Nava

Ship in a Bottle

No space,
I am cramped up,
My sails are small.
I have an anchor but no people.
All I can see is a blurry room with lots of books.
My flag has turned yellow,
The bottle is dusty
And the bottom feels as if it's falling out
But I am strong enough for a boy to use
As a toy.

The top is really special
For when a person looks at me
I get a gush of wind,
I think I am in the sun, sailing.
I have forgotten too many things.
There are hundreds of ships
Not like me.

Tara Byrne

The Ship in the Bottle

Standing in a glass bottle motionless
With only your thoughts running through your head.
The sun never sets in a glass bottle.
Only a faint glimpse of a boy
Sitting at a desk.
The dust settles on the glass bottle,
The dust of age.
An old man sits at the desk.

Katy Miles

Ship in a Bottle

No fish come to our net,
Our one and only ship in our world.
No cheers from the people
When we come to shore.
We make no profit from our job,
Only our souls' creator makes it.
No fish come to our net.

Sarah Hellier

13 PLACES AND DETAILS

This exercise is yet another way of concentrating the mind on details in order to present a vivid picture of a place to the reader. This method makes it a little easier for children to cope with and can lead to some good results.

The words *Town*, *Country* and *Seashore* are written on the board at the top, these will head three columns. The children are then asked to suggest as many things as they can think of which can be found in these places. All the words are written in a column down the board under the appropriate heading. The sort of things which they might suggest are contained in the lists below.

Town	*Country*	*Seashore*
bricks	hedges	rocks
roads	ditches	cliffs
street lamps	fences	sand
cars	animals	shells
shops	trees	seaweed
pillar boxes	grass	rockpools
telephone kiosks	streams	crabs
dust	barns	deckchairs
chimneys	farmhouses	donkeys
windows	drystone walls	gulls
street signs	lanes	boats
gardens	woods	sandcastles
kerbs	ponds	driftwood
pavements	birds	waves

These lists can be as long as you like, or as long as your blackboard! The headings are very wide but can be more specific if you wish. Other possible titles could be City Street, Parade of Shops, Market, Farm, Mountains, River, Village, Harbour, Underground Station. You could also do the same thing with seasons or months of the year. A good poem for showing the detail and feeling of a month is 'November' by Ted Hughes. You can also ask the children to make their own lists in their books rather than as a class.

The children are then asked to write poems using the words from the list so that they write one or two lines *only* on each item.

They must concentrate on a one or two line description of each thing and the whole poem will provide a detailed description of a particular place. The individual lines should be as interesting and vivid as possible and the value of this approach is that the children can pause to think after every one or two lines. The effort required for sustaining a long poem is broken down into manageable units. This also shows children one method of working, which is this layer upon layer approach. It is good practice for them to become used to making notes in this way before writing any poem. In their other writing they can always be encouraged to jot down quickly all thoughts and ideas on a subject and afterwards to select and order those which they wish to work on and improve for the final poem.

EXAMPLES

Suburbia

The roar of jets and trains rattles over old tracks,
Cars come to a halt at a zebra.
An old woman shuffles with her shopping
Crossing her prayers with kerbstones.
Outside her flat, a briefing with a neighbour,
Past her own screams she grudges babies,
Her shabby shawl limp on her shoulders,
Retired from her job she pumps on her pension.
Her lifeless card lies among lonely photographs
Her husband still alive in his uniform,
Daily she visits his memory,
While through her open window car fumes cloud.
Unfinished knitting on an armchair.

Ben Owen

The Beach

The beach is empty except for a sleeping few
Under cover, lying on lilos with punctures.
The low-water seaweed strangling the little fish,
The sand heavy with water from a weekend rainfall.
The ice-cream van with the yellow stripes
Is parked outside the town home
With its windows shut.
Empty deckchairs sunk in the ground.

Nicholas Midgley (YWW)

The Town

The smothered building on a page,
A castle with too many pictures behind it.
The factories still have their spirit.
Children scream while the milkman is not heard,
The trees will never reach their destination.
The milk clutters against the crate
To make our sound of life.
The dustmen will always belong
Like chess pieces on the move.

Debbie Stephens

Winter Seashore

Brighton beach wet, cold, damp,
Pier distorted in the sea,
The wind howling through a ghost train tunnel,
A witch stares a plastic stare.
Deck chairs form little pools
Where a tramp sleeps huddled against the cold.
The rain penetrates a sandcastle which has been
    defeated.
A lonely fishing boat chugs a tune over the silky sea,
A summer beach a postcard picture.

Jason Weir

Town

As feet wear away thought and time
The highrise flats watch
From high up on their cement thrones.
Street lamps line up
Like long regiments of soldiers
Their stems rooted to the ground.
The few trees that stand in huddled bunches
Slowly choking, their withered branches hang low.
The old alley cat playing in the dust,
A thick dusty bundle of fur and a slight purr.

Matthew Wevill

(See also 'Seashore', Chapter 17, page 74, and 'Seashore' Chapter 18, page 81.)

The Country

Tall trees guarding fields
Like soldiers on their watch towers.
Grass stalks stand in suspense,
A pigeon on a garden fence
Gently cooing as if reciting poetry.
A goat gnawing away
Through the remains of the past.
A robin hovering.

Matthew Wevill

Portland

Needles prick into the bloodshot eyes of the sky,
As the Race combs its white hair.
The rock bathes in the font of the sea,
Cleansing its skin,
Whilst its expression is held taut in malice.
Cries sing together from the prison on the hill.
Their hymn whispers in the long yellow grass,
And echoes in the open air chapel of the quarries.

Miles Greene (YWW)

The Cloud

The mountain reached up to touch the sky
With its white hand.
The cloud looked down upon the tired climbers
With the food on their backs
And their fame in their heads
And the flag up above them.

The ocean threw a wave at the sky,
The cloud watched the boat waddle through the water
With the sail in its chest
And the air in the sail
And the water slapping water.

The city threw smoke at the cloud.
The cloud watched the worker
With a grey-blue anorak
And his small packed lunch
And nothing else.

Nicholas Midgley (YWW)

14 SHELLS, PICTURES AND JACK-IN-THE-BOX

This is an exercise which has similarities to *Ship in the Bottle* (see Chapter 12) in that it partly involves putting oneself inside an object. It does more than that however as will become clear. It should be carried out as a class lesson and no preparation should be done. There is an element of surprise needed to ensure its success. Ideally the class should work in silence and fairly strict timing ought to be observed. Giving time limits in the way this exercise does will probably automatically encourage silent working – no time to talk. The exercise is taken step by step.

First of all the words *shell, picture, jack-in-the-box* (and any suitable objects which have an inside into which one might go in the imagination) are written on the board. Nothing is said about them but the children are asked to choose one word only and write it at the top of the page. Ask them to imagine a particular shell, picture, or jack-in-the-box.

They then have five to ten minutes *only* in which to write down a description of what their object looks like, starting with the words 'Outside the . . .' When the time is up everyone must stop. The next thing you ask them to do is to put themselves *into* the object and write for five to ten minutes on what that looks like, beginning with the words, 'Inside the . . .'

They should soon have built up a detailed picture of their subject which has made it their very own. They should now be ready to move on to the next stages which will take them out of the concrete and provide scope for a different kind of writing. Between each stage there is no discussion, no talking at all. This would interrupt and spoil the whole fantasy that is being woven.

The next piece of writing concerns the dreams of the jack-in-the-box, or picture, or shell and begins with the words 'My . . . dreams . . . ' The same time limit is set.

The fourth angle depends for its success on the atmosphere that has been generated. By now the children should be very involved in their subject and should feel a possessiveness towards what they have created. They are asked to give it away. What feelings would they have in doing this and what instructions, if any, would they give to the recipient? This section begins with the words, 'If I give my . . . to you . . .'

Having given it away they will probably experience a sense of loss or release. Either way can provide the substance of the fifth and final section which begins with the words, 'Without my . . .'

The exercise is now complete and the best thing to do is to hear everyone's piece. This could be regarded as a workshop and everyone encouraged to make comments both critical and complimentary about each other's work. This is best led by the teacher but as unobtrusively as possible. The teacher's place here, I think, is to 'head off' destructive criticism, and over-enthusiastic praise of friends' work or of things which are perhaps less worthy of it. Encouragement with discernment should be the theme and the teacher can perhaps enter the discussion to endorse a comment or to highlight a passage or phrase which is good but seems to have been overlooked. We do not want to discourage children in any way from being prepared either to venture opinions and constructive criticism, or to offer their own work for discussion by a class. The more children know about the writing of poetry, the better they will become at conducting workshops. If these are carried out in the right spirit the benefit that can be gained is enormous.

Some of the pieces written for this exercise might stand on their own without any more work, but generally what has been written serves as notes and a basis on which to do further work. It may be that one section is obviously better than the others and can be worked on to provide a poem. It may be that there is material for more than one poem. This exercise can show a way of working for the future, namely to write down quickly all the thoughts on a subject out of which a line will emerge which can be pursued.

EXAMPLES

Jack-In-A-Box

Outside the Jack-in-the-Box was the silent fright.
Inside the Jack-in-the-Box
The fright was in the making,
It forgot to frighten the millions.
The thoughts forgot it in its silence.
The box nerves broke open into loud realism.
The trap door opens
Into the mist of light,

Shouting brilliantly, sharp in laughter and
Screams.
As he swings free, hung by the neck,
Blue eyes set in pools of concrete,
Smiling he finds pleasure in his death.
Through the larder is carried the box,
The silent procession fights the crowds of age.
I gave this coffin to my past youth.
I cremated the box in the flames of my past time,
Lost in time.
My shadow found a place behind me,
The shadow loomed square
And three dimensional in its cubed glory.
The shadow wasn't mine.
It sulked away and was forgotten
As it had forgotten
How to frighten me.

Miles Greene (YWW)

Picture

Outside the picture the big golden rimmed frame,
The yellow flowered wallpaper
Leading down to the fireplace.
The curve-shaped hook to hold up a thousand
    thoughts,
The picture handed from century to century, glistening
    of tomorrow,
From side to side the canvas cracks and fades
As the house falls to decay.
The picture rises to brilliance.
Outside the picture the gold frame
With angels peeking over
Like the sun rising to bring new life.
The outside edge is as far as you can go,
If you go further you will fall into eternity.

Inside the picture the world is being held in three single
    colours
Rattling to escape.
The baby sitting in the corner waiting to be free
To grow and burst out.
The small squashed space to be cut
Into a million little stars to be shared by the world.

'Mother, mother,' the babe shouts out
But nobody can hear inside the ring of torture,
Nor in heaven can he be heard.
The plants never grow inside,
They are seeds for ever.

The picture dreams of fame from the world
Yet it is still stuck in an everyday room,
In an everyday house
Soon to crumble and dissolve.
Who can save it now?
Now that it is alone for ever,
Dreaming, yet always in reality.
The babe wants to grow and cannot,
The child's mind may comfort its round body
And yet do nothing to help.
'Mother, mother, come and make me famous',
    he dreams.

If I give the picture to you
How long would it survive?
Would the dream fade away for ever?
Will I be assured of the baby's care
Or will you leave him to die?
The question is, shall you take it
And never refuse to give it the fame it wants?
Is your mind set on the looking after
Of the diamond stone that never was found?
Can it survive without my mind?

Without my picture my brain is emptied
And will have to be filled with more things.
Who can care for a picture
When the world is falling apart?
I am falling apart as well
But I care not for myself
'Mother, mother,' the baby is still trapped.
The Mona Lisa laughs.

Nicholas Midgley

15 PARAPHRASE POEMS

I first came across this idea from the poet Vernon Scannell to whom the credit should be given. The idea is that the teacher takes a famous poem, but one which you hope the children do not already know, and writes a prose paraphrase of it. You should avoid using key words but aim to have all the information in the correct order. The completed paraphrase is then read out to the children, or written up on the board. If it is read out it may be necessary to read it at least twice while the children take notes. They are then asked to write a poem using all the information they have been given, and preferably in the same order. When they have finished they read their poems out to the group and the culmination of the reading is to hear the original poem.

There are many interesting sides to this exercise for teacher and children alike. Firstly, making a paraphrase of a poem can be quite difficult. One of the essential qualities of a poem is its economy of language. A paraphrase almost always turns out much longer than the original. This is a useful teaching point to show one of the differences between prose and poetry and to emphasise how the language of poetry is more highly charged.

Secondly, poetry in this highly charged manner uses words which can have more than one meaning. To communicate this in prose can tie you in knots even though in the poem you instinctively assimilate all meanings at the same time. Poems can also appear to say one thing and really mean another. I tried to paraphrase Stevie Smith's 'Not Waving But Drowning' and found it almost impossible without making the prose very clumsy.

Not being allowed to use key words from a poem forces you to search around for other ways of saying the same thing and very often this causes problems because there are no obvious alternatives. I find this very stimulating as an exercise and, of course, it makes you look at a poem much harder than you may have done before. You realise many nuances which previously may have escaped you and you can grow to appreciate the poem even more or look at an 'old faithful' in a new light. I suppose it could also put you off a poem too – but at least you would know what you were rejecting!

These are all aspects which I feel can benefit the teacher. For the children it is fun to hear the original and compare it with their own poems on the same subject. It is also a way of introducing them to good poems which ensures that they understand them and listen to them, and, probably, remember them. A good discussion can follow such a lesson, looking in detail at the original and appreciating the way the poet wrote about the subject in the light of their own poems.

An extension to this can be done by dividing the class into two or more groups. Each group can take a poem and paraphrase it in prose, with the help of the teacher if necessary. The groups can then exchange paraphrases and write poems of their own based on the paraphrase they have received. Neither group should know the original of the other and they can hear the results at the end. This teaches children to look at poems in detail but with another purpose in view, which is an added incentive, and links the reading of poetry (and what can be gained from that) with their own writing.

For adults, and perhaps for children too when they have had some experience of this, a kind of quiz game can be played which can be quite amusing. You take it in turns to paraphrase famous lines of poetry and the others must quote the original. This is not as esoteric as it may sound – most people know quite a few lines of poetry when it comes to it! You can introduce variations such as paraphrasing in dialects or particular accents. A travesty? No, just fun!

EXAMPLES
An attempt at a paraphrase of 'Adlestrop' by Edward Thomas, followed by children's poems, and, lastly, the original.

No, I'll never forget that small railway station.
It stuck in my mind because I was on an express
train which should not have stopped there at all,
but it did, one hot day after lunch, at the
beginning of summer.
I remember hearing the sound of steam
escaping from the valve and somebody coughed
or something. But there was just an empty
platform. Nobody got on to the train, or off it,
there was absolutely no-one about. I just recall
noticing the name of the station.
That was the only thing I saw except for a few
trees, some grass and a couple of different sorts

of wild flowers. There were also some small
stooks of hay standing about drying in the sun.
Everything was as still as the tiny clouds high up
in the sky.

Well, we only stopped for about sixty seconds
but somewhere, not far away, just then I heard a
particular bird singing and I felt as though I
could almost hear all the other birds there must
have been in that county and the next, singing
away as well, with him, off into the distance.

Poems

(a) Steaming through thirsty June countryside
My eyelids heavy, I doze.
A rush of steam, a moment's panic,
Have I missed my stop?
I lean out of the window.
A small dilapidated station,
A ringing silence.
Brambles guard an old bench with its peeling paint,
Hay spread out to dry, only attracting insects.
I wait for the bang of a door, the guard's whistle,
But only the uneasy silence.
And then a bird's song, strong and confident,
It fills the air and overtakes the silence.
All this packed into sixty seconds, deep in my memory.

Anna Cheifetz (YWW)

(b) It was the trans-continental express.
We stopped for a minute at the deserted station,
The engine let out steam and a mystery man coughed,
It was the cue for a strange bird to start singing.
The sound echoed amongst the dancing daisy patches
     and heather,
Even the firs, and the pines, along with the hay and
     grass,
Revolved to the bird's singing.
We were all lazy from our lunches
And the picturesque setting of the small high clouds
     was typical.
I shall never forget Ploines,
Though I couldn't find it on the map.

Robert Northcott (YWW)

(c)   *The Station*

It was a hot June day,
The express train drew to a stop.
I lazily looked out of the window,
Were we there already?
No, it was a peaceful country station
Where the train shouldn't have stopped.
The crimson poppies nodded in the sun
Making a patriotic combination
With the cornflowers and the cow parsley.
The prickly hawthorns stood crooked
At either end of the short station.
Nobody got on,
No-one got off.
The people in the front and back carriages
Didn't have a chance
Because the platform didn't stretch that far.
Then slowly, steadily, building up steam,
We left the station,
That little country station,
That I'll never forget.

Laura Bacharach (YWW)

And now for the original.

Adlestrop

Yes, I remember Adlestrop –
The name, because one afternoon
Of heat the express-train drew up there
Unwontedly. It was late June.

The steam hissed. Someone cleared his throat.
No-one left and no-one came
On the bare platform. What I saw
Was Adlestrop – only the name.

And willows, willow-herb, and grass
And meadowsweet and haycocks dry,
No whit less still and lonely fair
Than the high cloudlets in the sky.

And for that minute a blackbird sang
Close by, and round him, mistier,
Farther and farther, all the birds
Of Oxfordshire and Gloucestershire.

Edward Thomas

16 RENGA

This is a Japanese form of poem based on haiku – a seventeen syllable poem in three short lines containing five, seven and five syllables respectively. Renga, as I understand it, is a series of linked haiku. The second haiku takes as its subject something touched on in the first. The third deals with something mentioned in the second, and so on, creating a sort of chain of thoughts linking one haiku with the next. The final haiku (we make it the seventh) has to try to draw together in its three lines all the themes of the previous six. This is the hard part, needless to say.

We have tried writing renga in two ways, one more successful than the other. Firstly, it lends itself to a communal effort where each person writes a first haiku and then passes the paper on to the next person. The second haiku is then written and the papers passed on. This is repeated until the seventh has been completed. Seven people will have had a hand in writing these renga which can be extremely interesting. It does, however, make writing the seventh one very difficult. I cannot honestly say I have had much success with this approach with children.

The second way seems to be better, where each child writes his or her own complete renga. Whether you consider the following suggestion to be a cheat, or not, it is actually easier sometimes to write the seventh haiku first and work backwards. I do not see anything wrong in this approach but purists may differ. As an exercise I feel it is very valuable but should not be attempted before the children are familiar with, and practised in writing, haiku. (A fuller explanation of haiku can be found in my first book, *Does It Have To Rhyme?*) Any subject should be suitable, but it is perhaps easier to choose an overall theme (e.g. time, cats, food, the seasons) to run through the poem. Each haiku can then concentrate on specific examples which interlock, one verse with the next.

EXAMPLE

Renga

Perpetually ticks
Catching the moments of time,
The clock's hands move on.

The car moving on
Towards its destination
Of a place unknown.

Shrouded in darkness
Warriors knock at the door.
When will they come out?

The door made of oak
Has seen many visitors,
Some arrived at night.

In a veil of
Darkness a murder is done,
Mystery all round.

The man is prostrate
Stabbed to the heart, memories
Have caught up with him.

Messenger of fate,
The memories have murdered,
The clock is the cause.

Robert Northcott (YWW)

17 IAMBICS

When children do an exercise aimed at introducing or improving a technique of writing poetry, inevitably, in many cases, much of the spontaneity is lost. But if they wish to improve their handling of words and to add depth to their poetry it is essential that they should learn the craft of writing. Far from being a limitation in a bad sense, the use of various techniques can, in time, provide a release to the creative processes of the mind and produce better work. When the children are accustomed to differing forms they will find that what they want to say will somehow select its own form when they come to writing it down.

However, as with any other discipline, it is necessary to practise the techniques in order to understand their possibilities (and limitations) and to become thoroughly versed in how to use them. Therefore, although it may seem a little forced to introduce a technique for its own sake, it will lead to better things. It is like playing scales or learning tables – a certain degree of satisfaction is obtained from being able to do it and a great deal of useful knowledge is assimilated without which the children will never progress.

One of the ingredients of poetry is rhythm, and there are many different types of accepted rhythms quite apart from one's own personal rhythm, which everybody has. (Finding it is another thing!) One of the forms which interests me and which I find slightly more adaptable and easier on the ear, is writing in iambics. The rhythm of iambics can be illustrated as follows:

When I	do count	the clock	that tells	the time
They flee	from me	that some	time did	me seek

These two lines are in iambic pentameters which means they have *five* feet as shown by the dividing lines (rather like bars in music). Each foot contains two syllables, the first weak (un-stressed) and the second strong (stressed). The rhythm is best felt by reading the lines aloud. This is the rhythm used for sonnets. Iambic comes from the Greek ιαμβικος meaning 'limping'.

| ˘ 'Twas br͞íll | ˘ ĭg a͝nd | ˘ t͞he sl͞í | ˘ t͞hy to͝ves |
| ˘ H͞ad we͝ | ˘ b͞ut wo͝rld | ˘ ĕno͝ugh | ˘ a͝nd ti͝me |

These lines have only four feet but are written in iambic rhythm. You can find many examples of poems written in iambics which can be used as illustrations when introducing this form to children. You will notice often that small deviations occur in the rhythm of a predominantly iambic poem and this is good to point out to children. It shows, as with any technique, that when you have mastered it, you can legitimately afford to 'play around' with it to a certain extent. Sometimes it is necessary to vary the rhythm just a little to avoid a monotony of pace or to achieve a dramatic effect. If it feels and sounds right it should be acceptable.

Since iambic rhythm corresponds fairly naturally with English speech patterns this exercise is not too difficult to work and can, when used well, be reasonably unobtrusive and easier to write in than some of the more 'plonking' rhythms that people still sometimes associate with 'real poetry'.

One way of helping the children feel the rhythm is to spend a short time when everyone tries to speak only in iambics. This can be fun and after a very short while it soon becomes difficult to speak in any other way. This will help to ensure that the children are 'steeped' in the rhythm and understanding how to use it.

Another point worthy of mention is to encourage the children to run the lines on, that is not to make each line an entity of meaning in itself. This will vary the feeling of the rhythm and help to relieve the pattern. An example of what is meant here can be seen in the first poem below.

> I held him in my hand, his body limp
> And shaking, a cat watching all my moves.

The first line runs on naturally into the second. Punctuation can also be used for this effect.

EXAMPLES

The Dead Bird

> I held him in my hand, his body limp
> And shaking, a cat watching all my moves.
> I buried him, dead in his garden grave
> Where rain had fallen on his stone cold corpse

Like tears of crystal from an unknown friend.
I placed him in the grave and covered him
With soil – a lolly stick to mark the place.

Lucy Tizard (YWW)

The Strange Man

His will had said
To burn the bed,
To burn the chest
And all the rest.

The people said 'We disagree,
You must send it to charity.'
But the lawyer's word is good enough
And so they had to burn the stuff.

I watched the fire burning,
And the fire slowly turning,
For the creature of the air
Had claws to scratch and tear.

It reached out to devour me,
As if to show its mockery
The fire gave a bubbling roar,
Then it was black, and was no more.

Nicholas Midgley

Untitled

But I am always walking in the rain
To wash away all sighs and hopes of joy
And stamp out all the time I spent with you.
The sorrows cloud around me as I think,
Thinking of days when we prevented tears
But now the crying pain pours down on me
And slowly shrinks my heart to the size of yours.

Hedy-anne Goodman (YWW)

If I Should Die Before I Wake

If I should die before I wake
I leave my will to all of you.
My money and my profit take
But do not take more than you're due.

If I should die before I wake,
Take my home and take my land;
Share everything as I would wish
As it is written by my hand.

If I should die before I wake
I shall be free from all of you,
I do not care what you do now
For all my mortal days are through.

Nadya Kassam (YWW)

Death

If only sleep would come and with it peace
My mind would rest and bring me thankful dreams,
Yet all I do is twist and turn, I burn
With fever. Friends are gathered by my bed
Like vultures crouching here to watch me die,
Their claws are grasping, eyes alight with greed.
The room around me seems to spin with fear.
The door admits a blackness, shadowed death,
For is not shadow merely death's own slave
To clasp me close, to take me to the grave?

Megan Trudell (YWW)

Seashore

She crouched amongst the mounting hoards
Of seaweed, wood and cut rope cords,
Of white eyed fish washed on the beach
And bobbing buoys beyond her reach.
Her chubby hand lifted to feel
The battered boat's rough bite of steel
And felt around the water cool
Depressions made by the rock pools.
And feeling past the water's face
Her hand felt crabs in hard shell case,
And as she let her hand hang free
Her gaze flew out across the sea.

Tilly Ballantine (YWW)

18 SOME POINTS OF TECHNIQUE

This chapter deals with a few points of technique which can be used by children in their writing. Some of them have been mentioned in passing in other chapters but they are set out here for easier reference. They are points that the children should be constantly aware of and use as they feel necessary. They are tools in the craft of writing that will help to give shape to the children's poems. There are many examples illustrating these techniques throughout the book. I have chosen only a few to illustrate each point here.

Rhyme Patterns

Rhyme, when well used, will add music and rhythm to poems and assist in giving a form and polish to the finished work. It does not need to be a conventional rhyme pattern but can be the children's own invention. Near rhymes (e.g. *dine* and *done*) and spelling rhymes (e.g. *clover* and *plover*) can be used, and internal rhyme – within and not at the ends of lines – can also add texture to poems.

EXAMPLES

To Be Sold

Metal meets metal, the last noise.
Not seeing, only hearing the *rain*
Drill down on the corrugated *tin*,
The calf inhales the *smell* of his ancestors
Who know the place *well*
Like a criminal knowing his *cell*.
Winds play tunes through holes in the *walls*,
The orphan baby whose mother is gone
And she *calls*.

Zak Hall

House on the Horizon

House on the horizon,
Gaze back at *me*.
I see you sleeping,
Darkened, that I *see*.
Your little door is crying,
Your roof is not just *slate*.
I must never go near you,
For the thing that I would *hate*
Is the thought of getting closer
And not to touch the *gate*.

Nicholas Midgley

The Day They Walked Forever

That day when they walked down the hill,
The day when all the men were still
For it was fear now walking past,
When all the trees came alive at last.
The elders say 'It's but a dream'.
But the children saw it on the green,
The wooden figures that walked by
And floated slowly to the sky.

Nicholas Midgley

The Candle

A flickering light
Stunning and bright
Protruding into
The surrounding night.

A yellow flame
Sharp but tame
Like the shock of hair
On a lion's mane.

A cylindrical waxen figure,
A snow covered pole
Burning away slowly
It's no longer whole.

A familiar figure
Standing there
Alone in one room,
Solitaire.

Lincia Daniel (YWW)

Alliteration

The judicious use of alliteration in small phrases within a poem will add to the poem's success almost without the reader being aware of it if it is done subtly.

EXAMPLE from 'Suburbia' by Ben Owen (see Chapter 13, page 57, for the complete poem).

An old woman *sh*uffles with her *sh*opping
Crossing her prayers with *k*erbstones.

and

Her *sh*abby *sh*awl limp on her *sh*oulders,
Retired from her job she *p*umps on her *p*ension.
Her *l*ife*l*ess card *l*ies among *l*one*l*y photographs . . .

Metaphor

With similes, metaphors are almost a prerequisite of good poetry. In describing something the imagination draws parallels between one object or experience and another, which may be completely unconnected. Seeing these links and pointing them out to others is one of the joys of poetry and gives scope for original and creative thought.

EXAMPLES

Life is a Book

Life is a book lost for words,
Unfinished sentences
Standing on a page.
A bent staple clings to the paper,
The pencil waits to do
Its immortal full stop.

Charles De'Ath

Alcohol

Like a black cat it wanders into your life
Going round and round until the job is done.
A spiral of death mixing until smooth.
When you look at a book it reads you,
An eye peering at you,
Staring at you
From every corner, moving towards the middle.
The gun in your mind turns to fire,
The gun shoots death, the fire leaps.

Helen Alexander

Repetition

The use of repetition should not be overdone as it should be part of
the form of the poem. It might be used for emphasis or as a refrain
at the beginning or ends of stanzas. It may also represent a symbol
or motif which haunts the poem through repetition. The practice of
merely repeating the poem's first line as its last line, in some kind
of attempt to 'round it all off', is not one I would encourage.

EXAMPLES

Riddle

No man can enter
Without breaking in,
A small insect can die
And with ease
Get in.

No man can enter
Without breaking in,
No insect can exit
Already there.

No man can enter
Without breaking in,
An old insect there
Did it long before him.

Anna Colloms (YWW)
(Fossil)

Afraid

Evacuated from your town,
Leaving your homelife behind,
Being taken to an unknown destination.
Led away from my life's beginning
Never to see it again.
Pass through towns leaving weeping relatives.
We left in fear, we left in hope.

Our fathers have gone off to fight
To save our homes and our town.
We'll win, we say, We'll win, we say,
They'd never let us down.
We left in fear, we left in hope.

We left in grief
And not to be obliged
Hoping to see our families once more.
We left in fear, we left in hope.

Karen Bounds

From 'The Making of the Tiger' by Nadya Kassam (see Chapter 9, page 43).

The face and the staring eye
Seem to be alone,
Not with the body
The staring eye,
Not with the body
The motionless face,
The harsh silence.

Running on Lines

In order to vary rhythm and pace it is essential that children be made aware that lines of poetry do not have to be complete in themselves. The sense of a line can run from one line to the next and will help the poem to be freer. This point can also be emphasised to help the children's reading of poetry. Too many people still believe it is read line by line instead of noting sense and punctuation and reading it accordingly. The fact that it is written in lines and possibly in a particular rhythm will still come through but in a more natural way.

EXAMPLE

The World Reunion

Ladies and Gentlemen,
We are gathered here today
For me to say
About our plan
To run away.

Ladies and Gentlemen,
We have come here to leave
And not to grieve
For dead friends,
Don't deceive.

Ladies and Gentlemen,
You'll meet some you don't know,
Friendships will grow,
Some will not,
A counterblow.

We must forget our past,
Lock it in an iron cast
In our mind.
We will have no outcast,
We will not be classed
Above others.

We will have food to eat,
Our hearts will go at a steady beat
In our chests,
And anyone who tries to cheat
Or force others into defeat
Is banished.

We will be in the unknown,
But we will not be alone
Where we are,
And when lost we will be shown
To a place of our own
To rest.

Nicholas Midgley

Chain Writing

This is linked to repetition but is a little different. A word or phrase from one line is used to begin the next, and so on throughout the poem. (See also Chapter 16, *Renga*, page 69.)

EXAMPLE

Seashore

Pretty shells washed onto the sand,
Sand a golden yellow colour,
Colour in the blue of the sea,
Sea with gentle lapping waves,
Waves clouded with green seaweed,
Seaweed clinging to the breakwaters.
Breakwaters stand ugly in the water,
Water envelops the cliffs,
Cliffs with bare white faces.
Faces of donkeys and faces of people,
People lying tanned in deckchairs,
Deckchairs lying disregarded.
Disregarded boats tied to the piers,
Piers standing rooted in pebbles
Pebbles worn smooth by the water,
Water collecting in the rock pools.
Rock pools inhabited by limpets,
Limpets stuck to surrounding rocks,
Rocks distorted like bits of wood,
Wood washed up along the shore,
Shore with litter, synthetic rope.

Nadya Kassam (YWW)

Question and Answer

This is a form which can provide a pattern for a whole poem. It can be used as a conversation between two people. It is not a technique that should be used too often, but it has possibilities which the children might wish to explore.

EXAMPLE

The Worthless Form

What is the city's name?
The city has no name,
They don't care for history.
How do they live?
They live out of tin cans.
What keeps them alive?
They're kept alive by the turn of the cement mixer.
What is their aim?
Their aim is a future of skyscrapers and robots.
Where do they live?
They live in a city of dreams for the future
And hatred of the past.
What is their work?
Their work is to overpower reality.

Hedy-anne Goodman

Contradictions

This is one device that can be used to create a disturbing atmosphere or a surreal quality of the sort perhaps found in dreams where the opposite may occur to what you intend, or think is happening. For example, you are running as fast as you can but it is all in slow motion and you seem never to reach your destination.

EXAMPLES

The Dream

I see this world through my own eyes
– I cannot see myself.
Snow has found its way to this place,
It covers every side of the trees
And everyone here is old and wrinkled.
The whole place is silent and quiet,
This place feels deathly,
The old people aren't walking, speaking, working,
They just stand like figures in some horrific surrealist
    picture.
Their clothes and hair are still in the raging torrent of
    wind.
I fall further and further down
Before I hit the ground.

I wake with a jolt,
It is pitch dark in my room.
I cannot see my outstretched hand
Yet I know it is there.

Tilly Ballantine (YWW)

Similes

His smile was like that of a Cheshire cat,
His face was as solemn as the barren trees in winter.
That day his humour was more sarcastic than it had
   ever been,
His good news from abroad put him in a good mood.
His mind was as confused as a mad professor,
That day he was feeling fully aware.
On that Sunday morning, as on all Sunday mornings,
The streets were silent and free from all city bustle,
The crowds swarmed the shopping precinct
Like bees in a hive.

Lincia Daniel (YWW)

Economy of Language

Sometimes it is better for a poem to understate its case leaving the reader to think on for himself, and it is almost always true to say that in any poem there should be no redundant words. If you can omit a word or phrase without endangering the meaning and ways of effecting it in the poem then it is probably unnecessary. Every word must have a part (or parts) to play and a reason for being included. I feel this is perhaps one of the most important points to emphasise when encouraging children to write. To this end practice in writing haiku, tanka and cinquains is invaluable, and a constant purge on 'thens', 'ands', 'buts' should be in operation where these are unnecessary.

EXAMPLES

The Expectation of Death

A white painted room,
An ominous straitjacket,
A mental patient.

A train waiting room,
An old lady in her chair
Alone with many people.

Tilly Ballantine (YWW)

Wheelchair Feelings

I watch the boy with sympathy
Though I know nothing about him.
I watch his ugly face and deformed figure,
His smile an act of self-discipline.
The family grin into the camera.
For once he is not the lens,
For once they don't smile at him.

Hedy-anne Goodman

Style

Every child should be encouraged to find his or her own style, and as long as teachers do not impose their own ideas this should happen. There is no reason to interfere with what a child has written except to suggest that there might be better ways of saying a particular thing. One should never suggest how to do it or what to say. It is sufficient to say why something is *not* working and encourage the children to re-write it in another way. They must experiment for themselves. The more they have to take the initiative and discover for themselves, the better, so long as the teacher can back them up with informed criticism.

There are one or two things that ought to be said here. A poem does not sound more 'poetic' if too many adjectives or adverbs are used. Similarly, it is often better to use a verb in its proper form rather than overusing present participles. For example, the following extract from a poem contains too many 'ing' words:

Seagulls swoop*ing* over the rock*ing* waters
Gently mov*ing* the buoyant seaweed
As it stretches its slimy fingers
Reach*ing* for a dead crab
With one leg miss*ing*.
Bits of wood grat*ing* against the pebbles . . .

I would suggest that this can be immediately improved simply by changing some of the verbs.

Seagulls *swoop* over the rocking waters
Gently moving the buoyant seaweed
As it stretches its slimy fingers
To reach for a dead crab
With one leg missing.
Bits of wood *grate* against the pebbles . . .

I have heard of teachers who instruct classes to make sure they use two adjectives to describe each noun and include a lot of adverbs as this will make a poem 'better'. This is not true, it won't.

Another very important fundamental teaching point is to encourage children not to use a key word more than once unless it is for a specific purpose. If they think properly they can almost always find another way to describe what they want to say. It is lazy to use the same word over and over again – and this means virtually any nouns, verbs, adverbs and adjectives. Having to search for synonyms is good practice, enlarges the vocabulary and can often push the writer into new areas which otherwise may have remained unexplored.

19 LEARNING POEMS BY HEART

Once upon a time poetry was not written, but spoken. What memories our ancestors must have had, uncluttered as they were by the preoccupations of twentieth century living and the lumber of educationalists. Once upon a time poetry was a spoken art, closer to music, which could hold an illiterate audience spellbound for hours – something that might only apply to Shakespeare now, such is the limited attention span of fast-living modern society.

However, once upon a time, and not so long ago, we still spoke poems, at least in schools, under the laudable but misguided apprehension that it was 'good' for us to learn them off by heart. Do you remember the last-minute panic of memorising often unmemorable lines; the interminable mumbling and stumbling as one by one you stood to recite the *same* poem; the artificial choral speaking with flourishings of arms and voices? Too often this had the unfortunate effect of killing poetry for many people. How odd, I find, that usually the worst poems stay in my memory, word for word, and the best remain just a good feeling.

So, inevitably, there came the backlash and this practice of memorising has dwindled. A great majority of today's teachers came through the old system which did such a disservice to poetry. Most of my teachers at school were unaware of any poetry written since World War One and thus denied us the opportunity of relating to poetry through our own times. Of course, poetry speaks universal truths and I now love the work of poets throughout the centuries, but as a schoolgirl I would probably have welcomed more of a mixture of ancient and modern.

But poetry used to be spoken and enthral so why should it not do so again? Children learn songs easily, but there is also music in poetry. We have a strong oral tradition, kept alive in folk songs, rhymes and playground games, stronger perhaps outside the big cities but nevertheless there. People understand music and enjoy singing at all levels whether it be in the bath, pubs, amateur festivals or at professional standard. But poetry lost much of its appeal – writing, speaking, reading or listening – perhaps because of bad teaching in schools. The 'sixties and 'seventies did much to re-open this area and the success of public poetry readings has brought in a wider audience. 'A' and 'O' level courses now acknowledge modern writers such as Seamus Heaney and Ted Hughes, although poetry is still relegated to a tiny part of the curriculum. There are Art Schools, Music Schools, Drama Schools but virtually no Writing Schools A few groups and organisations run some courses but although competitions and writers' circles have revealed thousands of people who 'scribble away' in isolation, there is still reluctance to take poetry seriously or to recognise its importance. 'The pen is mightier than the sword', but try telling that to the government, or even to many teachers. However children of today do not have this induced antipathy towards poetry and perhaps the time is now ripe for its revival if we can learn from our mistakes. It all depends on how it is done.

I asked a class of ten-year-olds if they would like to learn a poem. I had my doubts but was overwhelmed by their response. They liked poetry and we had often read to each other poems which we had found in books. They were used to reading out their own work, too. Both practices had improved their reading techniques: good clear voices, expression with understanding, appreciation of poetry and discernment. They did this because they wanted to and gained in confidence each time. They were beginning to keep their own anthologies of favourite poems, writing them out in notebooks and illustrating them – another practice that has unfortunately almost disappeared. The idea of learning one was received with enthusiasm by most of them, particularly as they were given a completely free choice. There was no compulsion to do it which would have partly destroyed the enjoyment, and for the next few weeks odd moments every day were enlivened by children standing up to say their poems. About two thirds of the class participated and their choices were extremely varied and interesting. Some learnt more than one, and often the choices were astonishing. Some poems were complex and adult, perhaps not fully understood by the children and certainly not what a teacher might have considered setting for this age group, chosen for their 'music' with what can only be described as an intuitive sense of meaning and quality.

I felt it was important that I should learn one too, partly because it is not fair to ask children to do things you are not prepared to do yourself, and partly because I wanted to know what it felt like. I chose a favourite poem of mine and set to learn it one evening. It was surprisingly easier than I had thought and I went to bed excited by the words and the exhilaration of knowing and understanding the poem fully. A slight recurrence of the old conditioned nerves made me practise on a colleague at lunchtime and I recited it to my class that afternoon. I doubt whether they understood it but I am sure they appreciated my effort. I had put my head on the block too and I came away with a feeling of achievement unfamiliar for a long time. I think and hope their experience was similar to mine. We shall learn more. To be able to say a favourite poem to yourself, or quote whole passages which have meaning for you, can so often bring comfort and satisfaction.

20 HOW TO ORGANISE A WRITER'S VISIT

The points in this chapter are intended as a guide for teachers who would like to have a writer into school to read and talk to the children or to work with them. They are based on my own experience as a teacher who has organised such visits and also on the feelings of many writers themselves, most of whom have good experiences to relate, as well as horrifying tales of bad management by schools. These points, then, are an attempt to alert teachers, who may be thinking of arranging a writer's visit, to some of the details than can help to make it memorable and valuable for all concerned; the children, the staff *and* the writer. The value of arranging these visits is, I think, self-evident.

The Writers in Schools Scheme

The best way of arranging a writer's visit is through the Writers in Schools Scheme which was set up by the Arts Council in 1969 to assist schools to have writers in to read to, or work with, children. The fee and the date for a visit are agreed between the writer and the school and application is then made, at least three weeks in advance, for a subsidy towards the cost. The scheme is now operated by the Regional Arts Associations and a list of addresses and the areas served can be found on pages 99–101. Normally half the fee will be reimbursed to the school after the event and travelling expenses can also be reclaimed by the school. (Overnight accommodation, however, will not be covered.) Each region may operate the system slightly differently so it is advisable, in the first instance, to contact your local Arts Association. They should be able to supply you with a list of writers who are prepared to take part in the scheme, along with their addresses. If you want to approach a writer who is not on the list, check that this will be acceptable to your Arts Association. You should not be restricted to inviting only writers who live in your area. If you cannot find out a writer's address you can always write to him or her care of the writer's publisher.

Making Contact

Having chosen the writer you wish to ask to your school, write a letter of invitation, preferably offering alternative dates and with as much notice as possible to avoid disappointment. Do be adventurous in your choice of writer, even if you are a Junior School. Most writers will give a very good session with Juniors and it is well, particularly where poetry is concerned, to guard against only having writers who set themselves up as 'children's writers'.

If you know exactly what you would like the writer to do on the visit – read to the children and answer questions, run a workshop or give a talk about current literary trends etc – make this clear in your first letter. Also, if possible, state how large the group of children will be and how old. If you would like the writer to choose what kind of session it will be, then make this clear too. Suggest a fee – the minimum is stated by the Arts Association and this may be acceptable to the writer, or he may ask for a little more. It must be remembered that a freelance writer may have to give up two days of his working time to come to your school. Travelling one day, staying overnight and travelling back the next day can be very tiring when you do a lot of readings. This all interferes with a writer's own work. It is always good if you can persuade other schools in the area to engage his services too so that, for the writer, the trip is more worthwhile.

When the date, time and fee have been agreed write a letter to the writer confirming these and enclosing directions for finding the school, with details of arrangements for meeting him and overnight accommodation if necessary. Hotel bills must be borne by the school but in most cases you, or one of your colleagues, can probably put up the writer and this is normally quite acceptable. The next step is to apply for the subsidy to your local Arts Association.

Note: Do not expect your writer to work a whole day, or even a whole morning, for the standard fee. Too many teachers treat these visits as 'free periods'. Teaching is hard work and teachers are trained to do it. They also know the children. For a writer to be expected to do a full teaching day is most unfair, and the amount of time you expect the writer to 'perform' should be mutually agreed before the visit. He should also not be used merely as a convenient person to relieve Mr So-and-so of difficult classes so that he can put his feet up in the staffroom. Lastly, 9 am is perhaps not such a good time for a visit as, say, 11 am.

Preparing the Children for the Visit

Once the details have been fixed and you know which class, or classes, will be involved, some teaching preparation should be done. I feel it is essential for the children to know something about the writer and his work. They should have read or heard a number of poems by this writer (or one or two novels, or short stories) and any background information you are able to provide about the writer. It is far more satisfying for all concerned if the children know some of the work beforehand. The writer will be encouraged because, after all, writers want to be read – it is the work that matters – and the children will enjoy hearing poems read, which they already know, 'straight from the horse's mouth', as it were. They will find it easier to listen and to ask questions. Now is the chance to find out what he *really* meant by such and such a phrase. It will make what they have been taught come alive. They should be encouraged to make requests for poems they know by this writer to be read by him. They may want to show him some of their own although he shouldn't be bombarded with too much. Perhaps he can be presented with copies to take away.

If it is felt necessary a word about behaviour should be given in advance but try to avoid cowing them so that they dare not open their mouths. Make them excited about the visit in a positive and enthusiastic way.

Preparing the Room

Depending on what kind of session is to be conducted, give some thought to the ambience and conditions with which the writer will have to cope. For a reading in a classroom it is usually best to push back the desks and arrange the chairs in a semicircle. This will help to create as informal an atmosphere as is possible in a classroom. Make sure the writer has a good chair (not too low!) and a small table or something upon which to place his books. A carafe of water and a glass – the usual accessory for a visiting speaker – should be on the table too.

Try to choose a room, if this is possible, which does not have windows which many children from other classes will be passing. This can be very distracting.

If there are lesson bells and you cannot escape them please warn the writer in advance of when they are likely to sound and try to avoid children having to get up and leave in the middle of a session to go to another class. This requires tactful communication with other staff and departments on behalf of the children – do not put the onus on children to arrange to miss lessons as that is not fair. Whichever kind of room you have to use, try to make it as relaxed and informal an occasion as possible as this is probably best for everybody.

The Day of the Visit

Try to organise things so that you are available to welcome the writer on his arrival – failing that, at least make sure that somebody does. Allow time to sit down with a cup of coffee or tea, breathing space before the session.

The children should all be present in the room when you take the writer in. Make a short introduction and then, if possible, sit in the background so that your presence does not impinge on the children. If there is a time for questions be prepared to allow a silence to go on. The children may be shy at first but someone will usually open questions without the need for you to step in. If teachers ask all the questions the children can feel that they are excluded and will cease to be interested. The session has been set up for them and given the right preparation and opportunity they will certainly make good use of it.

When the session ends either you, or a child, should thank the writer and if you have established in advance that he will sign autographs then allow the children to line up. (This happens particularly in Primary Schools!)

It is best if you can arrange it so that the session ends a morning or an afternoon. Then the writer can be provided with some hospitality, if he wishes, in the way of lunch or a drink. Pubs or restaurants may be preferable to your school dinners but you can decide which seems best. One important matter now is to *pay* the writer. He should be paid on the day he visits – this is a ruling of the Writers in Schools Scheme. However, some schools *still* do not do this and I urge them to change this habit. Most writers who participate in this scheme are dependent on prompt payment in order to live. Making them wait, sometimes for months, seems to me to be merely bad manners. Even if the money is coming from your LEA it should be possible to arrange for payment on the day.

Selling the Writer's Books

This may not seem appropriate to do in school and I think the decision should be yours. I do not generally sell books to Junior Children at such times, although I might encourage them to buy from the local bookshop, which happens to be very good in our area, in advance of a visit.

However, many writers are able to bring along copies of their books to sell to the children, if you wish. This means that the children should be prepared for this and have money with them if they want to buy. It is better if you, or a colleague, can take charge of the selling to relieve the writer of any possible embarrassment and to free him to speak to the children. Your local bookshop may also be prepared to let you have copies on a sale-or-return basis, as do some publishers. If you have a school bookshop it might be persuaded to stock some copies. If the children have already bought some of the books they can, of course, ask the writer to sign their copies. Most writers are only too happy to do this.

I hope this chapter will prove of use to teachers who would like a writer to visit school. It can certainly be a very worthwhile experience for everybody and schools can build up valuable and lasting relationships with writers. I apologise if many of the things I have said seem to be only common sense but I have tried to cover most of the aspects and problems which I know have occurred from time to time.

21 THE ARVON FOUNDATION

This chapter deals specifically with one organisation which runs residential writing courses and I hope it will be self-evident how much value these can be to the children who attend them. School journeys have long been considered a marvellous way of extending the children in a different atmosphere to school, with its, of necessity, heavily timetabled day. The same sort of benefits are to be had from subject orientated courses, as these are, to those obtained from the more usual school journeys for physical recreation or environmental studies.

The Arvon Foundation was the brainchild of authors John Moat and John Fairfax who wanted to set up courses where people could get away from the pressures of everyday life and live for five days in the remote countryside to concentrate on writing. They began by setting up a few closed courses in various locations but in 1970 John Moat opened Totleigh Barton and Arvon had its first permanent home.

Totleigh Barton is an eleventh century thatched farmhouse said to have had associations with King John whose hunting lodge was nearby. It has been completely modernised and imaginatively furnished to provide accommodation for about fifteen students and two course tutors. There is central heating as well as romantic log fires for the winter months. The dining room boasts a very long refectory table which came from Woburn and there is a comfortable sitting room where readings and work sessions take place in a relaxed and informal setting. The kitchen is large and is generally the focus of the house where people naturally congregate for cups of coffee and conversation. The bedrooms have bunk beds and sleep two, three or four to a room, although there are one or two single rooms for those who feel they need them as well as for teachers who accompany school parties. One of the most interesting of these is the Monk's Room which was originally a priest's hole entered through the fireplace but is now approached by a staircase. It is said that the house has ghosts, but they are generally acknowledged to be benevolent!

The tutors are accommodated in a separate block known as the pigsties which adjoins the house, or in the goose house which stands separately facing the courtyard. There is also a large barn which has been converted to provide a workshop or performance studio for courses involving music or theatre. There are many quiet nooks and corners to which people can escape to write, as well as the beautiful Devon countryside. Totleigh Barton is close to the River Torridge (trout and Tarka country) and the nearest village is Sheepwash, about a mile and a half away. Okehampton is the nearest town, eleven miles to the south, and Bude is about twenty miles away.

During the summer months many 'open' courses are run on the lines developed by John Moat and John Fairfax and anyone can apply to attend one of these courses. All the courses, open or closed, cover mainly the writing of poetry, prose and plays, but there are also courses on painting, drama, writing for radio and television, music, folk song and video. Two tutors who are practising artists in the subject live alongside the students for five days and can be consulted at any time about the students' own work. The courses are reasonably free in organisation to allow the opportunity to provide what the students of each week might want. The sort of things which generally happen are as follows.

The tutors will give a reading of their own work; there is a visiting reader on one evening; course members read their own work in a special last evening performance; another evening is probably spent reading to each other poems by published authors found in the Arvon library; workshops may be held or sessions for stimulating writing through poetry games or discussion; the tutors are available for individual tuition regarding your own work and there is plenty of time and the right atmosphere to talk with others and to get on with your own writing. One day, usually the second, is traditionally allocated for sending the students out into the country in order to find ideas and the solitude necessary for writing.

During the winter months (October–April) the centre is available for schools, colleges and other organisations to book their own 'closed' courses for which they can choose the tutors and reader. I have taken many groups of children from the top Primary classes and have always found that they have benefited enormously, as do adults, from this extended contact with living writers. These are school journeys with a difference and the setting is particularly good for city children.

The domestic arrangements are deliberately informal. The centres are to be considered as 'home' for the week and all cooking is done by course members. This is not as horrific as it might first seem to some people. Breakfast and lunch are worked on a help-yourself basis. You can get up when you want and at any time of the day you are free to make tea, coffee, snacks, whatever you like, with the only proviso that you take account of other people. You do your own washing up – just like home! For evening meals a rota is usually worked out so that about four people take charge of cooking for everybody on one day only. The evening meals are taken together at the refectory table and are usually very convivial occasions. There are two centre directors at each place who are there to assist and advise. They will buy all the food you feel you need. In the case of school parties the teacher will have to organise the groups and perhaps help, particularly with younger children although they are quite capable of doing much of the cooking, but this side of the holiday is equally valuable and enjoyable for children. Learning to live together in a small community is all part of the experience and works very well. Do not be put off by what you might think sounds too much like 'commune' living – it is not really like that at all.

The other centre of the Arvon Foundation is Lumb Bank near Hebden Bridge in West Yorkshire – a very different setting with the Pennine moors and Haworth (Brontë country) not far away. The house belongs to the poet Ted Hughes who became involved with the Arvon Foundation in the early 'seventies and provided it with its second centre. It is an eighteenth century millowner's house in the land of millstone grit and is set halfway down steeply sloping pasture land on the side of the wooded valley of the River Colden which runs into the Calder. The valley contains the ruins of several silk mills which once thrived in the area. Now all that remains are the tall chimneys stubbornly straight against the sky while below the river rushes noisily over the rocks and falls, down to Hebden Bridge. The nearest village is Heptonstall half a mile up a steep track. This house has also been completely modernised and contains the same facilities as Totleigh, including a converted barn for workshops and performances. In winter the log fires add to the cheerful atmosphere of the living rooms and here, too, the long wooden refectory table helps to ensure that meals are enjoyable social occasions. The whole of one wall of the dining room has windows and a door giving access to the terrace and the magnificent views across the valley with the moors stretching away over the Pennines. (For a much better impression of this area than I can possibly provide here, see the book *Remains of Elmet*

(Faber) which has poems by Ted Hughes and photographs by Fay Godwin.) This dramatic landscape can, in any season, be particularly exciting for town children.

Lumb Bank

The frowning face of a person typing,
The wooden plaque's thoughts, orange in the flames.
Charcoal spreads laughs around the human library.
The poem is finished, the writing shadowed by
   happiness
And the cows' quiet footsteps under the buds of dusk.

Joanna Cooper

Devon

Devon brings you into an endless dream
Almost as if in a different world.
Fresh air fills your lungs
Like water filling an empty jug.
The sky so clear
You can see through it.
It seems that every house
You come across
Is filled with a sense of joy.
Every hill has wonders captured inside
For you to let out and set free.

Steve Webber

Both these centres are happy to take parties of children of about ten years and upwards, and many schools can already bear witness to the success of the venture. Those that have been to courses there usually go back again with new groups of children every year. If you are interested, and I can certainly recommend Arvon to anyone, I suggest that you visit one of the centres when a course is in progress, or, better still, go on an 'open' course first yourself, perhaps during the summer holidays. You can then see for yourself how it all works. The centre directors will be pleased to show you around and will be able to advise on suitable tutors for your requirements. They may also be able to tell you of schemes operated by some LEAs and Regional Arts Associations whereby you can obtain a subsidy towards the cost of the course for yourself or for the children. The costs are kept as low as possible, although affected by inflation, and compare very favourably indeed with courses run by other organisations. There is nothing quite like Arvon in the rest of the country and certainly nothing which caters for children as young as ten years old in this field. For further information write to one, or both, of the following:

The Centre Directors
The Arvon Foundation
Totleigh Barton
Sheepwash
Beaworthy
Devon EX21 5NS

Tel: Black Torrington 338

The Centre Directors
The Arvon Foundation
Lumb Bank
Heptonstall
Hebden Bridge
West Yorkshire HX7 6DF

Tel: Hebden Bridge 3714.

WRITERS IN SCHOOLS SCHEME

Regional Arts Associations (England)

Eastern Arts Association
Literature Officer
8/9 Bridge Street
Cambridge
CB2 1UA
(Tel: 0223 357596/7/8)

Bedfordshire, Cambridgeshire, Essex, Hertfordshire, Norfolk and Suffolk

East Midlands Arts Association
Literature Officer
Mountfields House
Forest Road
Loughborough
Leicestershire
LE11 3HU
(Tel: 0509 218292)

Derbyshire (excluding High Peak District), Leicestershire, Northamptonshire, Nottinghamshire, Buckinghamshire

Greater London Arts Association
Literature Officer
25/31 Tavistock Place
London
WC1H 9SF
(Tel: 01 388 2211)

The area of the 32 London Boroughs and the City of London

Lincolnshire and Humberside Arts
Literature Officer
St Hugh's
Newport
Lincoln
LN1 3DN
(Tel: 0522 33555)

Lincolnshire and Humberside

Merseyside Arts Association
Literature Officer
Bluecoat Chambers
School Lane
Liverpool
L1 3BX
(Tel: 051 709 0671)

Metropolitan County of Merseyside, District of West Lancashire, Ellesmere Port and Halton Districts of Cheshire

Northern Arts
Literature Officer
10 Osborne Terrace
Newcastle upon Tyne
NE2 1NZ
(Tel: 0632 816334)

Cleveland, Cumbria, Durham,
Northumberland, Metropolitan
County of Tyne and Wear

North West Area
Literature Officer
12 Harter Street
Manchester
M1 6HY
(Tel: 061 228 3062)

Greater Manchester, High Peak
District of Derbyshire,
Lancashire (except District of
West Lancashire), Cheshire
(except Ellesmere Port and
Halton Districts)

Southern Arts Association
Literature Officer
19 Southgate Street
Winchester
SO23 7EB
(Tel: 0962 55099)

Berkshire, Hampshire, Isle of
Wight, Oxfordshire, West
Sussex, Wiltshire, Districts of
Bournemouth, Christchurch
and Poole

South East Arts Association
Literature Officer
9/10 Crescent Road
Tunbridge Wells
Kent
TN1 2LU
(Tel: 0892 41666)

Kent, Surrey and East Sussex

South West Arts
Literature Officer
Bradninch Place
Gandy Street
Exeter
Devon
EX4 3LS
(Tel: 0392 218188)

Avon, Cornwall, Devon, Dorset
(except Districts of
Bournemouth, Christchurch
and Poole), Gloucestershire,
Somerset

West Midlands Arts
Literature Officer
Brunswick Terrace
Stafford
ST16 1BZ
(Tel: 0785 59231)

County of Hereford and
Worcester, Metropolitan
County of West Midlands,
Shropshire, Staffordshire,
Warwickshire

Yorkshire Arts Association   North Yorkshire, South
Literature Officer   Yorkshire, West Yorkshire
Glyde House
Glydegate
Bradford
Yorkshire
BD5 0BQ
(Tel: 0274 723051)

For details of schemes existing in Wales, Scotland and Ireland,
write to the appropriate Arts Councils:

Welsh Arts Council
Holst House
9 Museum Place
Cardiff
CF1 3NX
(Tel: 0222 394711)

Scottish Arts Council
19 Charlotte Square
Edinburgh
EH2 4DF
(Tel: 031 226 6051)

Arts Council of Northern Ireland
181A Stranmillis Road
Belfast
BT9 5DU
(Tel: 0232 663591)

Arts Council of Eire
70 Merrion Square
Dublin 2
Republic of Ireland
(Tel: 0001 764685)

SELECTED BOOKLIST

Anthologies	Editors
Over The Bridge (Kestrel)	John Loveday
Strictly Private (Kestrel)	Roger McGough
The Puffin Book of Magic Verse (Kestrel, hardback; Puffin, paper)	Charles Causley
The Puffin Book of Salt-Sea Verse (Kestrel, hardback; Puffin, paper)	Charles Causley
I Like This Poem (Puffin)	Kaye Webb
Worlds (Penguin)	Geoffrey Summerfield
Voices, the first book, the second book, the third book (Penguin)	Geoffrey Summerfield
Junior Voices, the first book, the second book, the third book, the fourth book (Penguin)	Geoffrey Summerfield
Touchstones 1, 2, 3, 4 and 5 (Hodder and Stoughton)	M. G. and P. Benton
Poetry Workshop (Hodder and Stoughton)	Michael and Peter Benton
Watchwords (series) (Hodder and Stoughton)	Michael and Peter Benton
Tapestry (Arnold)	Eric Williams
Dragonsteeth (Arnold)	Eric Williams
Telescope (Arnold)	Eric Williams
Looking Glass (Arnold)	Eric Williams
All Sorts of Poems (Angus and Robertson)	Ann Thwaite

Happenings 1 and 2 (Harrap)	Maurice Wollman and Alice Austin
Poems of the Sixties (John Murray)	F. E. S. Finn
Poets of our Time (John Murray)	F. E. S. Finn
Here and Human (John Murray)	F. E. S. Finn
The English Project, Stage One (6 books) (Ward Lock)	Various
The English Project, Stage Two (6 books) (Ward Lock)	Various
Wordscapes (Oxford University Press)	Barry Maybury
Thoughtshapes (Oxford University Press)	Barry Maybury
Bandwagon (Oxford University Press)	Barry Maybury
Bandstand (Oxford University Press)	Barry Maybury
Poems (series) (Oxford University Press)	Michael Harrison and Christopher Stuart-Clark
Round About Ten (series) (Warne)	Geoffrey Palmer and Noel Lloyd

INSIDE OUTSIDE

Sky with Diamonds (Macmillan)	Frank Plimmer
Fair on a Beautiful Morning (Macmillan)	Frank Plimmer
If I had a Hammer (Macmillan)	Frank Plimmer
Rhyme and Rhythm (Macmillan) Red Book Blue Book Green Book Yellow Book	James Gibson and Raymond Wilson
As Large As Alone (Macmillan)	Christopher Copeman and James Gibson
Soundings (Heinemann)	Kit Wright
First I Say This (Hutchinson Educational)	Alan Brownjohn

Volumes of Poetry	Author
Season Songs (Faber and Faber)	Ted Hughes
Rabbiting On (Armada Lion)	Kit Wright
Hot Dog (Kestrel)	Kit Wright
Once There Were Dragons (Andre Deutsch)	John Mole and Mary Norman
Mastering the Craft (Pergamon Press)	Vernon Scannell
Brownjohn's Beasts (Macmillan)	Alan Brownjohn
Salford Road (Kestrel)	Gareth Owen
CHATTO POETS FOR THE YOUNG (series) (Chatto and Windus)	Michael Baldwin Thomas Blackburn Leonard Clark D. J. Enright John Fuller John Heath-Stubbs Phoebe Hesketh Ted Hughes Brian Jones Edward Lowbury Gerda Mayer Clive Sansom Vernon Scannell R. S. Thomas

Further Useful Reading

The Practice of Poetry (Heinemann)	Robin Skelton
The Way To Write (Elm Tree Books/Hamish Hamilton)	John Fairfax and John Moat
Poetry in the Making – a teaching anthology (Faber and Faber)	Ted Hughes
The Dyer's Hand and other essays (Faber and Faber)	W. H. Auden
The Poet's Manual and Rhyming Dictionary (Thames and Hudson)	Frances Stillman